"From the recent flurry of studies on John C stand neither the sixteenth century nor oui Reformer of Geneva. This little book reveal. logian whose love for Jesus Christ and his church touches every area of human life. A jewel of a book!"

Timothy George, founding dean, Beeson Divinity School; general editor, *Reformation Commentary on Scripture*

"In a culture that applauds self-glory, and in a church that often appears to have forgotten its Christ, the work of John Calvin is as timely as when it was first penned. This wonderful book invites you into a theater of power, wisdom, authority, and grace, but it is not Calvin's theater; it is the theater of the glory of God in Christ. Here you will be thankful for the man Calvin and how he enables you to see life-shaping truths, but you will be even more thankful for Calvin's Christ. For as is true of Calvin, is true of every follower of Jesus, the faint glory of the man is only as good as it humbly and relentlessly points you to the spectacular glory of his Lord. Which is, in fact, the lasting legacy of the man this book remembers."

Paul Tripp, President, Paul Tripp Ministries; author, *What Did You Expect? Redeeming the Realities of Marriage*

"Contemporary interest in John Calvin and his writings has stimulated a widespread renewal in Reform theology and with it has created considerable controversy regarding stereotypical perceptions of Calvinism. Speakers at the 2009 Desiring God National Conference made a significant contribution to these issues by focusing on practical aspects of John Calvin's life and writings. These messages, edited by David Mathis and John Piper in *With Calvin in the Theater of God*, will be a blessing and encouragement to the reader in discovering an often neglected aspect of this influential theologian."

Jerry Rankin, President, International Mission Board, Southern Baptist Convention

"Sadly, for many Christians John Calvin has become more of a theological caricature than the real-life man of passion, reason, and pastoral concerns that he was. Fortunately, this is a book that tears back the curtain and allows us to see and understand the key intersections where his theology and his everyday life collided and then merged into the passionate love for Scripture and zeal for upholding God's glory that became his calling card."

Larry Osborne, Pastor, North Coast Church, Vista, CA

"These distinguished contributors do not seek to exalt John Calvin. But they rightly recognize that Calvin's ministry helps us exalt Jesus Christ. Follow them into the theater of God and behold the glory of the One and Only."

Collin Hansen, editor at large, *Christianity Today*; author, *Young, Restless, Reformed: A Journalist's Journey with the New Calvinists*

"In an age where Scripture is on the periphery in so many pulpits and man is glorified in so many churches, we desperately need this book. It reminds us not only of the great life and work of John Calvin, but most importantly the supremacy of the Scriptures and the glory of God."

Britt Merrick, Lead Pastor, Reality Carpinteria/Ventura

"What does a theologian and his theology look like if he and it are firmly centered on the triune God and his glory? These essays will show you. You will meet Calvin the pastor, the theologian, the polemicist, the husband, the father, the sufferer, the lover of God and his church—all roles played out in "the theater of God." Whether you're meeting Calvin for the first time or spending time with an old friend, this book will give you a glimpse of the wide horizons that are opened to one who has God's glory firmly at the center of life. Be warned, Calvin's vision is contagious."

Stephen J. Nichols, Research Professor of Christianity and Culture, Lancaster Bible College

"The authors of *With Calvin in the Theater of God* present us with a world-changing vision of God's glory that has profound ramifications for the practical realities of everyday life. Here we find proof again of that old axiom, *'There is nothing more practical than sound theology.'* I highly recommend it!"

Steven L. Childers, President and CEO, Global Church Advancement; Associate Professor of Practical Theology, Reformed Theological Seminary, Orlando, FL

"*With Calvin in the Theater of God* takes Calvin out of the ivory towers that many people mistakenly believe he lived in and shows how his robust theology played out in the practical life of a pastor attempting to care for his people. It shows how his belief in the sovereignty of God allowed him to suffer often, and suffer well, throughout his life. It shows how his hope in heaven allowed him to deal with the relentless stress and pressures of leadership. But most of all, this book shows what God can do through one man who's eyes are fixed, not on what we can see, but what we can't see, the things that are eternal. It inspired me to do the same as a pastor, husband, father, and man."

Jason Strand, Teaching Pastor, Eagle Brook Church, Lino Lakes, MN

"No theologian, living or dead, has been more influential in my ministry than John Calvin. Reading *With Calvin in the Theater of God* reminded me why. Each essay contributed something helpful both to my understanding of Calvin's life and ministry and to my affection for the Savior that Calvin relentlessly served. Whether you're a long-time student of Calvin or brand new to the Reformed universe, I highly recommend this book."

R. W. Glenn, Pastor of Preaching and Vision, Redeemer Bible Church, Minnetonka, MN

"As a church planter in New Orleans, I am continuously confronted by the destruction of this world's depravity. My primary counter-attack is to present a biblical vision of the glory of God in Christ. John Piper and my good friend David Mathis have compiled an amazing work displaying Calvin's biblical vision of God's redemptive glory."

Rob Wilton, Lead Pastor, Vintage Church, New Orleans, LA

"For a generation of Calvinists who seem to know little about Calvin himself, this is a timely book. By taking us straight to the heart of Calvin's everyday life and ministry, the authors introduce us to Calvin the pastor and expose us to the daily grind of his pastoral work and personal suffering that shaped and informed his teaching and writing. Calvin's voice can be heard throughout the book, exhorting us to live our lives "with one foot raised," ready for the day God wills our departure from this world. This book left me with a hunger to taste and trust God more, and in the end, truly honors Calvin by pushing our thoughts and worship past him and to the true hero of God's theater and Calvin's ministry, Jesus Christ."

Beau Hughes, Campus Pastor, The Village Church, Denton, TX

"As a young pastor with less than a decade of experience, I desperately need the wisdom of faithful pastors who have gone before us. I have found in these pages much needed, refreshing, and challenging insights for the daily grind of ministry life. Lest we forget the divine glory that is shot through this "grand stage," Calvin—through his life and his writings—pulls back the veil of seeming routine to reveal it once again in all its splendor. And the authors of this brief volume you hold in your hands serve as worthy guides and fellow stage-hands with the old master in the theater of God. Read on, and behold again—in all things—God's radiant glory."

Matthew Molesky, Pastor for Preaching, Calvary Community Church, St. Cloud, MN

"In this book you will meet John Calvin the pastor, apologist, evangelist, church planter, Bible teacher, theologian, and pilgrim. The version of Calvin you get from his enemies, and sadly even from some who claim to be his friends, is a hammer-headed, abstract bore. The real Calvin, and the theology he proclaimed, is the opposite. His life and ministry reflect the clearest message of Jesus and the deepest message of the Bible—the grace of God to sinners, for the glory of God."

Justin Holcomb, Director, the Resurgence; Adjunct Professor of Theology, Reformed Theological Seminary

"These writers are not just historical spectators observing John Calvin's life. They are participants in the theater of God with Calvin, and they want you to participate in that theater by embracing the truth that drove Calvin: God's glory is demonstrated preeminently through Christ, revealed to us through the Word, and manifested in our everyday life. This volume points you back to the unfolding drama of God's kingdom."

James H. Grant Jr., Pastor, Trinity Reformed Church, Rossville, TN

"*With Calvin in the Theater of God* is a rich and readable introduction to one of the church's greatest pastor-theologians. Examining Calvin from many angles—including pilgrim, counselor, public intellectual, and sinner—the contributors offer an elegant composite of the man even as they point to the object of his worship and work: Jesus Christ. It is perhaps the resolute faithfulness of Calvin's life that most stands out here; this steadfastness, which in God's providence produced a major Christian movement bursting with energy today, reminds us that our faith is exercised hour by hour, day by day, trial by trial, all for the honor and acclamation of the Lord. Whether eminent or unknown, we are reminded in these pages that in the grand theater of God's glory, there are no bit players."

Owen Strachan, coauthor, *The Essential Edwards Collection*

"The great glory of God revealed in all things is the Copernican Revolution for anyone seeking to live everyday life in an extraordinary way. John Calvin's addiction to this view of God is worth studious exploration. David Mathis and John Piper's *With Calvin in the Theater of God* is without a doubt a must read for those new to Calvin and looking for an introduction to the Revolution, or for those who are in need of another beautiful and freeing drink from the tavern of God's sovereignty."

Steve Treichler, church planter and Senior Pastor, Hope Community Church, Minneapolis, MN

"If Calvin intrigues, inspires, or even baffles you, then you'll want to get this latest contribution to his teaching ministry and life. This work digs through five hundred years of history and unearths one of the church's greatest treasures—the heart and mind of John Calvin—and places it not behind the walls of academia but on the pulpits of pastors and in the pews for laymen. Applying the brilliance of Calvin to the hardest theological questions and the most stubborn challenges of everyday Christian-living, this book will enlighten you with the great breadth of Calvin's biblical worldview."

Robert S. Scott Sr., Pastor, Los Angeles Community Bible Church; general editor, *Secret Sex Wars: A Battle Cry for Purity*

"These writers are not just historical spectators observing John Calvin's life. They are participants in the theater of God with Calvin, and they want you to participate in that theater by embracing the truth that drove Calvin: God's glory is demonstrated preeminently through Christ, revealed to us through the Word, and manifested in our everyday life. This volume points you back to the unfolding drama of God's kingdom."

James H. Grant Jr., Pastor, Trinity Reformed Church, Rossville, TN

With Calvin
in the Theater of God

WITH CALVIN
in the THEATER
of GOD

THE GLORY *of* CHRIST *and*
EVERYDAY LIFE

GENERAL EDITORS
John Piper *&* David Mathis

CONTRIBUTORS
Julius Kim, Marvin Olasky, Sam Storms,
Mark Talbot, Douglas Wilson

:: CROSSWAY
WHEATON, ILLINOIS

Library of Congress Cataloging-in-Publication Data
With Calvin in the theater of God : the glory of Christ and everyday life / general editors, David Mathis and John Piper ; Contributors Julius Kim . . . [et al.].
   p. cm.
   Includes bibliographical references and indexes.
   ISBN-13: 978-1-4335-1412-8 (tpb)
   ISBN-10: 1-4335-1412-5
   ISBN-13: 978-1-4335-1413-5 (pdf)
   ISBN-13: 978-1-4335-1414-2 (mobipocket)
   1. Calvin, Jean, 1509–1564. 2. Reformed Church—Doctrines.
I. Mathis, David, 1980–   . II. Piper, John, 1946–   . III. Kim, Julius.
BX9418.W58   2010
230'.42—dc22   2010011673

Crossway is a publishing ministry of Good News Publishers.

VP		19	18	17	16	15	14	13	12	11	10
14	13	12	11	10	9	8	7	6	5	4	3	2	1

In Memory of
JOHN CALVIN
Fellow in the Theater
Wearer of the Spectacles
Lover of the Savior

CONTENTS

Calvin is a cataract,
a primeval forest,
a demonic power,
something directly down from the Himalayas,
absolutely Chinese,
strange,
mythological;
I lack completely the means,
the suction cups,
even to assimilate this phenomenon,
not to speak of presenting it adequately. . . .
I could gladly and profitably set myself down
and spend all the rest of my life just with Calvin.

KARL BARTH
to EDUARD THURNEYSEN, 8 June 1922;
in *Revolutionary Theology in the Making: Barth-Thurneysen
Correspondence, 1914–1925*
(Richmond: John Knox Press, 1964), 101

CONTRIBUTORS

Julius J. Kim is dean of students and associate professor of practical theology at Westminster Seminary in Escondido, California, as well as associate pastor of New Life Presbyterian Church in Escondido. He received a BA from Vanguard University; MDiv from Westminster Seminary; and PhD from Trinity Evangelical Divinity School. Julius directs the Center for Pastoral Refreshment dedicated to helping sustain pastoral excellence among Korean-American pastors. He is author of *The Religion of Reason and the Reason for Religion: John Tillotson and the Latitudinarian Defense of Christianity, 1630–1694* and contributed to *Covenant, Justification, and Pastoral Ministry: Essays by the Faculty of Westminster Seminary California*. Julius and his wife, Ji Hee, have two daughters.

David Mathis is executive pastoral assistant at Desiring God and Bethlehem Baptist Church in Minneapolis, Minnesota. He grew up in Spartanburg, South Carolina, graduated from Furman University, and came to the Twin Cities with the collegiate ministry Campus Outreach, with whom he ministered at the University of Minnesota and Northwestern College. He is a graduate of the Bethlehem Institute (now Bethlehem College and Seminary), a distance MDiv candidate at Reformed Theological Seminary, Orlando, and an elder at Bethlehem's downtown campus. David has written articles and chapters for various publications, but this is his first published book. He and his wife, Megan, are the parents of twin boys Carson and Coleman.

Marvin Olasky is editor-in-chief of *World* magazine and provost of The King's College, New York City. He earned a BA from Yale University in 1971 and a master's and PhD in American culture from the University of Michigan in 1974, 1976. From 1978 to 2008, he worked at the DuPont Company and was a professor at The University of Texas at Austin. Marvin has written twenty books as well as two thousand articles for publications ranging from *World* to the *New York Times* and the *Wall Street Journal*. He is an elder of the Presbyterian Church in America, and he and his wife, Susan, have four sons.

John Piper is pastor for preaching and vision at Bethlehem Baptist Church in Minneapolis, Minnesota, where he has served since 1980, seeking to "spread a passion for the supremacy of God in all things for the joy of all peoples through Jesus Christ." John has written over forty books, including *Desiring God; The Pleasures of God; Don't Waste Your Life; Seeing and Savoring Jesus Christ; What Jesus Demands from the World; God Is the Gospel;* and most recently *Think: The Life of the Mind and the Love of God.* John and his wife, Noël, have five children and an increasing number of grandchildren.

Sam Storms is senior pastor at Bridgeway Church in Oklahoma City, Oklahoma, and president of Enjoying God Ministries. He is a graduate of the University of Oklahoma (BA in history) and Dallas Theological Seminary (ThM in historical theology) and received his PhD from the University of Texas at Dallas. In addition to over thirty years of pastoral ministry, Sam taught theology and historical theology at Wheaton College for four years and is author of many books and numerous journal articles. Sam and his wife, Ann, have two grown daughters and two grandsons.

Mark R. Talbot is associate professor of philosophy at Wheaton College, where he has taught since 1992. He earned his PhD in philosophy at the University of Pennsylvania. His areas of academic expertise include philosophical theology, philosophical psychology, David Hume, Augustine, and Jonathan Edwards. Mark has published many book reviews, magazine articles, and chapters in collaborative volumes. He is married to Cindy and has one married daughter and three grandchildren.

Douglas Wilson is pastor of Christ Church in Moscow, Idaho. He is a founding board member of Logos School, a senior fellow of theology at New St. Andrews College, and an instructor at Grayfriars Hall, a ministerial training program at Christ Church. Douglas helped establish the Confederation of Reformed Evangelical Churches (CREC), edits Credenda Agenda (www.credenda.org), and has authored numerous books on classical Christian education, the family, the church, and the Reformed faith. After serving in the U.S. Navy in the submarine service, he completed a BA and MA in philosophy and a BA in classical studies from the University of Idaho. Douglas and his wife, Nancy, have three children and a bunch of grandkids.

TIMELINE OF CALVIN'S LIFE

1509, July 10—Born in Noyon, France, to Gerard and Jeanne Calvin.

1517, Oct. 31—Martin Luther nails his Ninety-five Theses to the church door in Wittenberg (Calvin age eight).

1523—Departs with two of the Montmor sons for the University of Paris (age fourteen) where he would learn Latin from Mathurin Cordier and become aware of Wycliffe, Hus, Luther, and the ongoing Reformation; he would earn a BA and MA in Paris.

1528—At his father's request, goes to Orléans to study law (almost a year), then to Bourges (three years); surrounded by the best of humanism but felt little admiration for it; converted sometime between 1528 and 1532.

1529—Luther and Swiss reformer Ulrich Zwingli meet at Marburg, agreeing on every point of doctrine but the Lord's Supper.

1531—Calvin's father, Gérard, dies; Calvin returns to Paris (age twenty-two).

1532—Writes his first book, a commentary on Seneca's *De Clementia* (age twenty-three).

1533—Sixteen years after Luther's Ninety-five Theses, Nicolas Cop delivers controversial All Saints' Day convocation address that heralds Christ as the sole mediator (not any "saints"); many alleged it was written by Calvin.

1535, Jan.—Goes to exile in Basel.

1535, May—Geneva becomes a Protestant city.

1536, March—Published first edition of the *Institutes* from Basel.

1536, Summer—Leaves Basel to travel to Strasbourg for secluded study; Hapsburg-Valois war forces him to reroute through Geneva for one night; convinced to stay in Geneva by William Farel.

1537, Jan.—Calvin and Farel begin their work in Geneva in earnest.

1538, April—Farel and Calvin expelled from Geneva; Calvin goes first to Basel, then to Strasbourg for the happiest three years of his life (his "golden years").

1540, Aug.—Married Idelette de Bure, widow with two children, Jacques and Judith; they would be married almost nine years until her early death.

1541, Sept. 13—Reenters Geneva; would stay in Geneva until death.

1542—Plague comes to Geneva; Calvin stays to care for his congregants; only child born and dies.

1548—Wife of Antoine (his brother) imprisoned on suspected adultery and soon released; convicted nine years later of adultery with Calvin's manservant.

1549, Spring—Death of Calvin's wife, Idelette.

1549—Union of the Swiss Reformed churches under the Consensus of Zurich, drawn up by Calvin and Heinrich Bullinger.

1553–1554—"The fateful years" when according to T. H. L. Parker "two large storms blew from different quarters and raged simultaneously. The one was the decisive battle with the libertines; the other (of which they were glad to make use) the Servetus affair."

1553, Sept. 3—The day when Libertine named Berthelier was to return to the Table and Calvin took his stand; would prove to be the deathblow for the libertines.

1553, Oct. 26—Servetus condemned to be burned; burned the following day.

1558—Calvin very ill during the winter of 1558–1559; thought he was about to die.

1559—Denis Raguenier begins taking down Calvin's sermon notes.

1559—Academy of Geneva established; definitive edition of *Institutes* published.

1564, May 27—Dies at Geneva; as requested, buried in an unmarked grave.

INTRODUCTION:
Divine Glory & the Daily Grind

David Mathis

Five centuries have passed since John Calvin walked the streets of Geneva. If you would have passed him along the way, you could have recognized him as the thin man wearing a strange cap (so the artists tend to think) and carrying a Bible (the Book that changed everything for Calvin, and has something to say about everything). And if you greeted Pastor Calvin and extended your right hand, you might be surprised.

Don't only notice his smile and the pastoral warmth in his eyes, but as he raises his hand to yours, see if you can catch a glimpse of his fingernails. If so, you'll see the dirt—maybe not what you were expecting. Geneva's pastor may have wished in early adulthood to keep his hands clean with a quiet life of ivory-tower study, but the dream never became a reality. He was instead divinely consigned, for his own good and for ours, to everyday life in the real world where the rest of us live—the life of pain and mess, disorder and emergency, sin and suffering, dirt and grime.

THE PLEASURES AND WORRIES OF DOMESTICITY

Church historian Stephen Nichols writes,

> Calvin is often understood out of context, as if he formed his ideas and established his particular take on doctrine, what we call Calvinism, in utter isolation from other people and cut off from the world around him. The picture most have of Calvin is a lone gun turning ideas over in his head in his ivory tower. This couldn't be further from the truth.[1]

The Calvin home was no scholar's paradise. Biographer T. H. L. Parker notes that "for most of his life Calvin's house was full of young children."

---

[1]Stephen J. Nichols, *The Reformation: How a Monk and a Mallet Changed the World* (Wheaton, IL: Crossway, 2007), 71.

He "passed his life, not in the seclusion of a monastery or in humanistic quiet but in the midst of the pleasures and worries of domesticity," and so his famous *Institutes* "was not written in an ivory tower, but against the background of teething troubles."[2] Added to that, Calvin was "not unfamiliar with the sound of the mob outside his house threatening to throw him in the river and firing their muskets."[3] He kept his fingers dirty with everyday life.

EVERYDAY LIFE: ORDINARY AND GLORIOUS

But we should be quick to note that Calvin's subjection to the daily grind did not prove to be an obstruction to his view of the divine glory. On the contrary, the difficulties of the everyday—his "light momentary affliction" (2 Cor. 4:17)—were used by God to open Calvin's spiritual eyes and to enable them to see more beauty and more light.

> We might be tempted to say that, when Geneva claimed him [as its pastor], the Reformation was throwing away its greatest writer. And so, in one way, it was. He had inevitably less time to give to study and to the polishing of his sentences with the City Council worrying him about drains and heating apparatus, with ecclesiastical quarrels to settle with other Churches and worries and sickness in his own home. But, in fact, he could hardly have written so voluminously if he had been allowed his quiet life in Strassburg or Basel.[4]

It was the everyday life of suffering that produced his holy angst, the everyday life of disorder that begged for his arrangement, the everyday life of deadlines that prodded his productivity. It was an everyday life surrounded by distraught souls needing encouragement and deeply depraved sinners needing help with holiness. He simply would not— *could* not—have done what he did had he been tucked away in studious solitude, trying to maximize his isolation from the world and its fallenness. Quarantined from the church, he would have been little good to her.

EVERY INCH

Under the relentless pressures and pains of everyday life, Calvin came to see the truth and comfort of the absolute sovereignty of God over all

[2]T. H. L. Parker, *Portrait of Calvin* (1954; rep., Minneapolis: Desiring God, 2009), 80.
[3]Ibid., 41.
[4]Ibid., 47.

things and in all things. *All things* is not a throwaway phrase—for the apostles or for Calvin. *All things* means there is a lifetime of laboring to be done—and more—in discovering the full-orbed gloriousness of the gospel in the Scriptures and then applying it to everything. Calvin was twenty-five years younger than Luther, and the Reformation was already making its initial world-changing surge as Calvin came into adulthood. But the emerging Reformation triumph of divine revelation over human reason would need a lifetime of investment to merely begin developing the implications—implications for everything.

Calvin did not operate as a speculative philosopher, leaning on his own mind, but as a biblical theologian, leaning on God's revelation in the Bible. He sought to live out *sola Scriptura*, not merely ascribe to it, endeavoring to make room for all the texts, including the big ones, the *all things* texts. He believed that God "works *all things* according to the counsel of his will" (Eph. 1:11) and that "from him and through him and to him are *all things*" (Rom. 11:36).

In the Book That Changed Everything, Calvin discovered that in Jesus "*all things* were created, in heaven and on earth, visible and invisible, whether thrones or dominions or rulers or authorities—*all things* were created through him and for him" (Col. 1:16), and that for those who are Christ's, "*all things* work together for good" (Rom. 8:28). The God of the Scriptures was no tribal deity. Every inch of the universe was his. Calvin's all-encompassing theology came from such big texts, and to believe them he had to read them. Taking God at his word in the Bible meant seeing that God relates to everything, and everything to God. It was in drawing on this strain in Calvin that his spiritual descendant Abraham Kuyper would claim memorably almost four centuries later that there is not one square inch in all the universe over which the risen Christ does not declare, "Mine!"

A WORLDVIEW WITH WINGS

Long before pastors and Christian college professors were saying this and that about the Christian worldview, Calvin was living it. Led by the Scriptures, he rethought as much of reality as he was able, consciously appropriating God's revelation of himself in the Bible and in the person of his Son. In a day when many saw human reason and divine revelation as equals, the Reformation principle of *sola Scriptura*—not Scripture as the *only* authority, but Scripture as the *only ultimate* authority—changed everything for Calvin. It captured him as a reality so massive that it would take more than a few weeks and a quiet place of study to work out its implications. It was a whole-life project for the everyday.

Relating God to everything did not mainly summon Calvin the scholar to retreat, but Calvin the pastor to advance, to take forward God's revelation into the everyday realities of cradle and grave, weddings and funerals, providential crossings along the road, home visits, appointments, classes, sermon preparation, meetings, family devotions, and daily chores. It did not exclude quiet study; it just called for more than mere study. Everything can be studied, Calvin saw. Everything relates to God.[5]

EVERYDAY ACTIVITIES TO GOD'S GLORY

We find this all-encompassing view of the world as God's world in all of Calvin's theologizing, with the hard doctrines he is best known for—like predestination, election, and God's exhaustive sovereignty—being no exception. Scott Amos writes,

> [F]or Calvin, God's sovereignty is not an abstract concept; it is vividly concrete, and it undergirds Calvin's understanding and perception of the world and our place in it. Because of this, God's sovereignty has immense practical value for Christians and for our worldview. Because of God's providential control of all creation, Christians can live confidently and engage in everyday activities to God's glory.[6]

LOCKING THE CHURCH DOORS

Calvin so believed in the importance of the everyday activities of Christian life and mission that he had a strange but telling practice in

---

[5]To press home the expansiveness of Calvin's all-encompassing worldview, note the Reformer's aggressive orientation toward "new media" as well as his continued effects on literature today. David W. Hall, in *The Legacy of John Calvin: His Influence on the Modern World* (Phillipsburg, NJ: P&R, 2008), draws attention to "Calvin's wise employment of the latest technology" (36), saying, "If Martin Luther seized on the potential of the printing press, Calvin and his followers elevated the use of the press to an art form. With the rise of the Gutenberg press, Reformers seized the new media with a vengeance to multiply their thought and action plans. Perhaps no first generation Reformer seized the moment quite like John Calvin" (33). Pulitzer Prize winning novelist Marilynne Robinson is a modern-day manifestation of Calvin's legacy in literature. The February 2010 *Christianity Today* article that referred to her as a "narrative Calvinist" calls John Calvin "a figure Robinson has been working hard to restore. In her preface to *John Calvin: Steward of God's Covenant* (2006), Robinson bristles at the fact that the Reformer has been hidden under a caricature, known only as 'an apostle of gloom dominating a gloomy city,' his legacy one of 'repression and persecution.' Robinson instead finds . . . liberating themes in Calvin's thought . . . [that] impress upon her literary vision" (Thomas Gardner, "Keeping Perception Nimble," *CT*, February 2010, 32–33).
[6]Scott Amos, "The Reformation as a Revolution in Worldview," in *Revolutions in Worldview*, ed. W. Andrew Hoffecker (Phillipsburg, NJ: P&R, 2007), 230.

Geneva. He was eager to see Jesus' church gathered on Sundays, but he was not happy for his flock to retreat from everyday life and hide within the walls of the church during the week. So to prod his congregants to be fully engaged in their city of Geneva—in their families, in their jobs, with their neighbors and coworkers—he locked the church doors during the week.[7] It must have been hard not to get the point. He knew the place of God's people—gathered together to worship on Sunday, but during the week not hidden away behind thick walls of separation, but on mission together in God's world, laboring to bring the gospel to metro Geneva in their words and actions, in all their roles and relationships.

ASTOUNDING PRODUCTIVITY

Calvin's expansive view of God's sovereignty, combined with the depth of his security in God's grace, produced an astounding drive to productivity in both himself and those he influenced. Many have called it "the Protestant work ethic." It may be counterintuitive at first. The natural mind thinks that motivating great exertions of effort requires withholding the reward. Work first for God, then get acceptance from him later.[8]

But the Christian gospel does precisely the opposite. By faith the Christian is connected to Jesus first and foremost, fully accepted by God, before being required to do anything (only to believe, which is itself a divine gift, Eph. 2:8; Phil. 1:29). Amazingly, such radical grace transforms, and thus frees, the Christian to exert great intensity and zeal in the cause of gospel good. Such transforming and freeing grace produces a man like Calvin so energized for doing good that as he lay dying in bed for weeks, he continued to dictate substance and letters of encouragement to others until only eight hours before his passing, as his voice finally gave out.

EVANGELISM AND MISSIONS

Some of Calvin's critics do what he didn't do and turn from truth revealed in Scripture to extrapolating by reason that God's sovereignty destroys

---

[7]Nichols, *Reformation*, 79–82.
[8]Calvin writes about Protestantism, in contrast to his childhood Catholicism, as "a very different form of teaching . . . not one that led us away from the Christian profession, but one which brought us back to its fountainhead, and by, as it were, clearing away the dross, restored it to its original purity." Cited in Parker, *Portrait*, 34.

the impetus for evangelism and missions. This may be one of the worst caricatures of all. Church historian Frank James is right to call "the real John Calvin . . . a man with a strong evangelical heart." Standing on the shoulders of significant new research, James says, "Far from being disinterested in missions, history shows that Calvin was enraptured by it." Additionally, "If Calvin is taken as a model, Reformed theology ought to produce not only the best theologians, but also the best pastors and missionaries. These convictions reveal the true Calvin behind the image."[9]

CALVIN AND MARTYRDOM

Noteworthy in this regard is Calvin's correspondence with many on the brink of martyrdom. Not only did he himself risk his life in France by embracing the Protestant gospel, but he became the spiritual father of many who did.[10] Here we see his fervent commitment to missions and his gut-wrenching entrenchment with the difficulties of everyday life. Calvin wasn't merely into "comfortable" missions; he knew that not only is suffering part of everyday life in this fallen world, but it often is the very means the sovereign Christ employs in building his church.

T. H. L. Parker may tell the story best. He writes that the persecuted French Protestants "looked up to [Calvin] not only as their chief pastor but as a father. When he writes to them, a particular note of affection creeps into his letters."[11] In 1553, Calvin wrote to five young French Protestants imprisoned in Lyons and condemned to death by burning:

> We who are here [in Geneva] shall do our duty in praying that He would glorify Himself more and more by your constancy, and that He may, by the comfort of His Spirit, sweeten and endear all that is bitter to the flesh, and so absorb your spirits in Himself, that in contemplating that heavenly crown, you may be ready without regret to leave all that belongs to this world.

---

[9]The quotations from Frank James are taken from his article "Calvin the Evangelist," in *Reformed Quarterly*, Vol. 19, No. 2/3 (2001), available online at http://rq.rts.edu/fall01/james.html (accessed 2-1-10). Similarly, Philip Hughes claims "irrefutable proof of the falsity of the too common conclusion that Calvinism is incompatible with evangelism and spells death to all missionary enterprise." Philip E. Hughes, "John Calvin: Director of Missions," in *The Heritage of John Calvin*, ed. J. H. Bratt (Grand Rapids, MI: Eerdmans, 1973), 40–54, quoted in Ray Van Neste's article "John Calvin on Evangelism and Missions" in *Founders Journal*, available online at http://www.founders.org/journal/fj33/article2.html (accessed 2-1-10). The fuller exploration of this issue will be in a forthcoming volume to be published by Crossway, tentatively titled *The Great Commission Vision of John Calvin* by Michael A. G. Haykin and C. Jeffrey Robinson Sr.
[10]Iain Murray writes, "Calvin never hid from those to whom he preached that believing the truth could well be their preparation for prison and martyrdom. Not without reason has it been said that Calvinism is a message for hard times." Iain Murray, foreword to *John Calvin: A Heart for Devotion, Doctrine, and Doxology*, ed. Burk Parsons (Orlando, FL: Reformation Trust, 2008), xiii.
[11]Parker, *Portrait*, 121.

He renewed the correspondence a month later:

> Since it appears as though God would use your blood to seal His truth, there is nothing better for you than to prepare yourselves for that end, beseeching Him so to subdue you to His good pleasure, that nothing may hinder you from following whithersoever He shall call. . . . Since it pleases Him to employ you to the death in maintaining His quarrel, He will strengthen your hands in the fight and will not suffer a single drop of your blood to be shed in vain.[12]

STUDYING AS HE COULD

In all this emphasis on the troubles of the everyday, we shouldn't think that Calvin had an aversion to study. His love for the Savior translated into an unquenchable appreciation of the preciousness of Jesus' making himself known in Geneva some fifteen hundred years after his death and resurrection, through the Bible, by the power of the Holy Spirit. Calvin knew that if his study of the Book waned, so also his vision of the divine glory, and with it his people's vision, would be gone. Calvin gave himself as he could to study—study that never felt like enough, study that was frequently distracted and often interrupted, but genuine study nonetheless. It was from such study that his world-changing vision of the divine glory and its ramifications for everyday life emerged.

There was a rhythm to Calvin's life, a rhythm of retreat for study and return for shepherding, of seeing the divine glory while struggling with the daily grind. This is what awaits us in the pages ahead. We won't find a Calvin who only studied and wrote, and we won't find a Calvin who only went from one noncontemplative activity to the next.

ENTER THE THEATER

We invite you to join us with Calvin in the theater of God. In his *Institutes*, Calvin talked about our everyday world as a "glorious theatre,"[13] "this most beautiful theatre,"[14] "this magnificent theatre of heaven and earth replenished with numberless wonders,"[15] in which we see God display for us his divine glory in all the hues and textures of daily life in

---

[12]Ibid., 122–23.
[13]John Calvin, *Institutes of the Christian Religion*, 1.5.8.
[14]Ibid., 1.14.20.
[15]Ibid., 2.6.1.

redemptive history—and climactically in the life, death, and resurrection of our story's Hero.[16]

In the theater of God's universe, Calvin is our fellow, not the ultimate Guide. Any guiding he does is toward the Guide of the Scriptures. According to Calvin, it is the Scriptures that are our spectacles, enabling us to really see the drama with proper clarity and import. And so Calvin warns us that "while it [benefits] man seriously to employ his eyes in considering the works of God, since a place has been assigned him in this most glorious theatre that he may be a spectator of them, his special duty is to give ear to the Word, that he may the better profit."[17] The Book is our Guide and unique lens.

As we enter with Calvin, our aim is to look at the world through the biblical specs, with Pastor Calvin adjusting the focus. This should not be a mere academic pursuit, but intensely practical—practical in the right ways. The chapters ahead are not full of tips and techniques and little how-tos, but the aim is unfolding the beauty of the central truths about God, his Son, and his world that affect everything.

Calvin's big, biblical vision of God changes everyday life. If you really want to be practical, don't reach for gimmicks, checklists, and self-helps, but come with Calvin to the Bible and get to know the most important realities in the universe: God, creation, sin, heaven, hell, Jesus, his cross and resurrection, the Holy Spirit. The biblical vision of the glory of God in Christ is the most practical reality in the universe.

THE PLAYBILL

The six chapters ahead lay out for us some of this all-encompassing worldview. There is here more Bible than Calvin—just the way he'd like it. In the chapters ahead, you'll see Calvin's rhythm of study and suffering, preparation and practice, sight of the divine glory and the unavoidable setting of the daily grind. We begin with a summary on Calvin's life and ministry, then work through five seriously theological and surprisingly practical chapters. In each we'll see doctrine bursting with everyday

---

[16]Timothy George writes, "Calvin believed that God had not only placed an innate awareness of Himself within all persons but had also revealed Himself in the wonders of the external creation as well. He saw God as a Worker (*Opifex*) who had displayed 'innumerable evidences' and 'unmistakable marks of his glory' in the whole workmanship of the universe (*Inst*. 1.5.1). Indeed, the universe was 'a sort of mirror in which we can contemplate God, who is otherwise invisible.' Or, to change metaphors, it was 'a dazzling theater' on which the glory of God shone (*Inst*. 1.5.8)." Timothy George, *Theology of the Reformers* (Nashville: B&H, 1988), 190.

[17]*Institutes*, 1.6.2.

repercussions, and we'll lift the theological hood to see the engine that drove Calvin's world-changing practice.

Julius Kim

First is Julius Kim's creative overview of Calvin's life and his telling of why he cares about the man John Calvin. Despite the considerable differences of time and culture, Julius identifies in a special way with Calvin's pilgrim life. In stride with Calvin's rhythm of studying God's Word and shepherding God's people, Julius takes us on a two-stop journey through Pastor Calvin's life and ministry. Here we see Calvin as a faith-possessed pilgrim with a singular passion to know God and to make him known.

Mark Talbot

After Julius sets the stage, Mark Talbot writes the first of five amazingly practical chapters—maybe not practical like you're used to, but practical in the everyday-life legacy of Pastor Calvin. Mark does serious business with our messes, the mess of fallenness in our world and the mess of fallenness in us. Mark writes as one who is no stranger to either rigorous study or real suffering. He profoundly knows the Calvin-like rhythm of eternal perspective and everyday life, and we get the immense benefit of years of thinking and living in this chapter. The mere theoreticians among us will be gently corrected, the sufferers greatly comforted. (Mark also carefully addresses the infamous execution of heretic Michael Servetus, and Calvin's role in it, in appendix 1 at the end of the book.)

Douglas Wilson

In chapter 3, Douglas Wilson goes right to the heart of what made Calvin to be Calvin: his extraordinarily high view of the Scriptures. Calvin worked out the principle of *sola Scriptura* more consistently than many of his fellow Reformers, and the implications were world shattering. As Doug shows us, it meant a remarkable understanding of preaching that produced astonishing power for world change.

Marvin Olasky

Next Marvin Olasky tackles Calvin on public life. It is mind-boggling to follow the political growth of the seeds Calvin sowed and the benefits millions enjoy today because of them. Calvin wasn't afraid to challenge conventional wisdom. In Calvin we find unexpected resources for Christians in government and as entrepreneurs.

Sam Storms

Having addressed sin, pain, preaching, and public life, Sam Storms challenges us to live, like Calvin, with one foot raised, ready for heaven. Far from "pie in the sky by and by," we'll see that having one's head in the biblical clouds is essential to being of real earthly good. Sam picks up on the pilgrim and suffering refrains and shows us why heaven will be heaven, and how meditating on the glory and joy to come gives the practical power for enduring unjust suffering, overcoming worldliness, and responding well to loss and rightly to death.

John Piper

In the final chapter, John Piper brings us to the dénouement of the divine Son—the grandest of all possible finales. John shows us that the theater of this world is not big enough, and old enough, to be the full theater of God's glory. He addresses God's ultimate aim of all that he does in the universe and closes with five practical observations.

TO FAN YOUR FLAME

Calvin was born July 10, 1509, just over five hundred years ago. This book got its start when our six contributors gathered in Minneapolis, Minnesota, on September 25–27, 2009, with a couple thousand friends to thank God for Calvin's life and ministry. The goal was not mainly to honor John Calvin, but we saw his five hundredth birthday as an occasion to honor God. And to the same end, we've assembled this book.

As with John's short biography *John Calvin and His Passion for the Majesty of God*, our "unhidden and unashamed aim in this book is to fan the flame of your passion for the centrality and supremacy of God"[18] in all things—with so many of the all things being the everyday things. If you missed the party in 2009, here's your chance to celebrate with Julius, Doug, Mark, Marvin, Sam, and John. Have your Bible handy.

---

[18]John Piper, *John Calvin and His Passion for the Majesty of God* (Wheaton, IL: Crossway, 2009), 12.

In the cross of Christ, as in a magnificent theater,
the inestimable goodness of God is displayed before
the whole world. In all the creatures, indeed,
both high and low, the glory of God shines,
but nowhere has it shone more brightly than in the cross,
in which there has been an astonishing change of things,
the condemnation of all men has been manifested,
sin has been blotted out,
salvation has been restored to men;
and, in short, the whole world has been renewed,
and every thing restored to good order.

JOHN CALVIN
Commentary on the Gospel According to John,
trans. William Pringle
(London: Calvin Translation Society, 1847;
repr. Grand Rapids: Baker, 1981), 2:73.

1

AT WORK AND WORSHIP IN THE THEATER OF GOD:
Calvin the Man & Why I Care

Julius J. Kim

At twelve years of age, Kim Gwan Hae became a pilgrim. Born into an aristocratic family in South Korea in the 1930s, Kim led a privileged life—he had the best clothes, the best food, and the best education. In fact, he did not have to go to school, but the tutors came regularly to his home. And all of his extended family lived with him, as was the custom. He and his family lived in the main house, while the relatives and cousins lived within the large compound. When I recently interviewed him, I asked him what he remembered most about his childhood. His answer surprised me.

"I don't really remember much of my home, or my clothes, or my tutors. What I remember are my mother's cries."

His father, out of a sense of shame for not being able to bear more children, regularly beat his mother in drunken rage. This continued for years such that his mother's fingers became permanently mangled from trying to stop the blows.

As he got older, unable to bear it, he would rush to his mother's room trying desperately to keep his father from beating his mother. But he only ended up getting beaten himself. This came to a climax when he turned twelve. He woke to the smell of fire burning in the home. The little house in which he and his mother now lived was on fire. He ran outside only to be confronted by his father holding the torch.

His father simply stated, "Leave now or die."

Kim replied, *"What are you talking about, Father? What are you doing? Have you gone mad?"*

The extended family and the other villagers rushed to see if they could help. But as they saw Kim Gwan Hae's father holding the torch, they could only watch, because they themselves were overcome with fear. Kim's father was not only the police chief of the village—the largest and most intimidating man with the largest sword—but he was also the richest man and often supported the villagers with money, food, and clothes.

Kim Gwan Hae could only watch as his mother gathered whatever she could and then came to grab his hand. With tears streaming down his face, Kim was banished from his home and was now a homeless pilgrim.

*   *   *

In his early twenties, John Calvin became a pilgrim. Having embraced the Protestant faith, Calvin had to flee his home and country and spent the rest of his life outside his native France. It is this pilgrim perspective that helps us understand Calvin the man and his work. Who was John Calvin? What motivated him? *John Calvin was a faith-possessed pilgrim with a singular passion to know God and to make him known.* In this brief introduction to the life and thought of Calvin, my goal is that you as a Christian pilgrim journeying by faith through the wilderness experiences of your life will also be able to taste and see the same grace and glory that thoroughly transformed this sixteenth-century Christian pilgrim.

TWO STOPS ON OUR JOURNEY

We will be making two stops as we journey back in time through Calvin's life. First, we will take a look at Calvin's education and early experiences to see how they shaped his view of and relationship to God. This stop will be called, "Knowing God: Calvin the Student and Scholar of the Word." Calvin was a man deeply committed to knowing God, especially as he revealed himself in his Word. He was convinced that the core of our worship of God and work for God must be based on the Word of God. As a lifelong student of Holy Scripture, Calvin committed himself to the daily and diligent study of the Word of God, and it was in this Word that he came to know the depths of his own sin and the power of Christ for his salvation and how to live as a pilgrim in this sin-cursed world.

The second stop along our journey will reveal how Calvin's study of God's Word formed his view of God and the ministry. This stop is entitled, "Making God Known: Calvin the Shepherd and Servant of the Church and the World." Calvin became a man passionately committed to making his God known through his work as a shepherd of the church and a servant of the world. The endless hours Calvin spent in his study of the Word had this clear purpose: to make God known through his life and ministry. Whether in a church of French refugees or a city council meeting before political leaders, Calvin committed himself to revealing the will of God as it applied to all areas of life.

KNOWING GOD: CALVIN THE STUDENT AND SCHOLAR OF THE WORD

John Calvin was a faith-possessed pilgrim with a singular passion to know God and to make him known. The passion and skill that Calvin was later to display in his writings and in his ministry developed over the course of his life. After a brief look at Calvin's education and conversion, we will examine his major work, the *Institutes*, which provides us with the two main themes that Calvin would pursue as a student and scholar of the Word: the sufficiency of Scripture and submission to what the Scriptures principally taught.[1]

Education

Born into what we might call a middle- to upper-middle-class family, Calvin received the privilege of being educated in the medieval system of the *trivium*, or the three ways or three parts of grammar, logic, and rhetoric. All of this was part of his father's plan to prepare him, like his older brother Charles, for the priesthood. His father, however, soon had a change of heart and directed his son John to forgo his preparation for the priesthood and instead switch to a career in law. As a result, Calvin dutifully studied at prestigious schools in France for four to five years. This momentary detour provided young John not only with a sharpening of his mind, but also an introduction to the Renaissance pursuit of the ancient sources of learning. God would use this training for his own glory, as we shall soon see.

---

[1]Biographical information on Calvin is based on the following sources: Theodore Beza, *The Life of John Calvin* (Durham: Evangelical Press, 1997); William Bouwsma, *John Calvin: A Sixteenth Century Portrait* (Oxford: Oxford University Press, 1988); W. Robert Godfrey, *John Calvin: Pilgrim and Pastor* (Wheaton: Crossway, 2009); Bruce Gordon, *Calvin* (New Haven: Yale, 2009); T. H. L. Parker, *John Calvin: A Biography* (Louisville: Westminster John Knox, 2007); Herman J. Selderhuis, *John Calvin: A Pilgrim's Life* (Downers Grove, IL: InterVarsity, 2009).

Renaissance learning captivated young John as a student of the classics. He especially admired the top scholars of the day known for their incisive commentaries on ancient sources. One such man was the great Renaissance scholar Erasmus. Calvin desired to follow in the footsteps of Erasmus by becoming a student of the ancient classics. Calvin's first published book was a commentary on *De Clementia* by the ancient Roman Stoic philosopher Seneca. Published when John was only twenty-three years old, it showed great promise and revealed Calvin to be a careful and insightful interpreter. Again, God was clearly preparing him for the great commentaries he would later write.

Conversion

As the story goes, Calvin did not remain a student and scholar of the classics. Something happened that utterly transformed his life, vision, and calling. Simply put, it was his conversion. He would come face-to-face with the Lord of glory, and he would never be the same again.

While we don't know the exact date, it was during this season of university studies that Calvin came into a vastly new understanding of Christianity. Unfortunately, there is not much information regarding his own journey from being a loyal son of the established church to eventually becoming a rootless pilgrim of the Protestant movement. What we do know is that his conversion is the key event that moved him from just being a student and scholar of the classics to being a student and scholar of the Word. Now the prime motive of Calvin's existence came to be "zeal to show forth the glory of God."[2]

It appears that his conversion happened quite suddenly, surprising Calvin himself. He came to recognize the seriousness of his sin and the need to look outside himself for a solution.[3] The solution came with help from the writings of the early Reformers like Luther, who many of Calvin's friends already were reading and studying. Here he came face-to-face with the depth of his own sin, the terrifying judgment of God, and the fact that the Roman Catholic Church did not have an adequate solution. So sometime during his twenties, Calvin became gripped by the power of the gospel as it was presented within the context of a church in dire need of reform.

---

[2]John Calvin and Jacopo Sadoleto, *A Reformation Debate*, ed. John Olin (New York: Harper, 1966), 58.
[3]Selderhuis, *John Calvin*, 19–20.

His conversion also signaled a new period in his life—a period marked by fleeing the religious persecution of his native France. Unable to stay safely in France, Calvin became a fugitive on the run, seeking a better home. His pilgrim life had begun.

Institutes of the Christian Religion

Calvin's conversion also marked another significant event in his life: the writing of his first major Christian book, *Institutes of the Christian Religion*. It was time to use all the training as a student and scholar to know God and to make him known.

Though he wanted to spend the rest of his life as a student and scholar of the classics, to sit and read for long hours studying, analyzing, and writing, Calvin knew that it was one thing to know God more and quite another thing to make him known, especially as he became increasingly aware of the necessity for the reform of the church. With the *Institutes*, Calvin would transition from being a student-scholar of the world of the classics to a student-scholar of the Word of God.

First written in 1536, *Institutes* was his introduction to the Christian faith. In fact, this first major Christian publication not only reveals what was central to his life and ministry but also provides an outline of the major themes that Calvin would spend his life developing—key themes like the sufficiency of Scripture and the submission to the Scriptures, especially in the areas of salvation and worship.

The book was relatively short, consisting of only six chapters. But it reveals the heart of what Calvin thought was vital not only to the cause of the Reformation but more importantly for the way it prepared disciples for Christ and his church. Chapter 1 described the law and the gospel, that is, the knowledge of sin and salvation. Chapter 2 was about faith, specifically how one is justified by faith alone. Chapter 3 covered prayer and the importance of communion with God. Chapters 4 and 5 dealt with true and false sacraments, that only the Lord's Supper and baptism were valid sacraments instituted by Christ. Lastly, chapter 6 outlined how the Christian is free in matters of religion from all human innovations since he is bound only to Scripture.[4]

Calvin would go on to revise and expand his *Institutes*, but this first

---

[4]John Calvin, *Institutes of the Christian Religion, 1536*, trans. F. L. Battles (Grand Rapids, MI: Eerdmans, 1986).

attempt made it abundantly clear what Calvin considered of primary importance not only for true religion but also for the reformation of false religion. "Calvin made it clear that Christ, faith, justification, the sacraments, and the Scriptures stood at the heart of his understanding of Christianity."[5]

Why did he write the *Institutes*? The dedicatory letter to King Francis I of France gives us a clue. In it he appealed to the king not to listen to the lies of his enemies but to see the real purpose behind the vision for reform. Calvin was distressed because his enemies were charging that the Protestants were revolutionaries trying to overthrow the peace. These lies, according to Calvin, had caused the persecution of many of his fellow Protestants. So in order to protect Protestants, and also to present what he considered true religion, Calvin wrote the *Institutes*.

So, as a student and scholar of the Word of God, Calvin emphasized two main themes: the sufficiency of Scripture alone for faith and life as well as submission to what the Scriptures taught.

SOLA SCRIPTURA: SCRIPTURE ALONE

What were the key elements of his program of reform? First and foremost, Calvin argued that the Bible, and the Bible alone, was the ultimate foundation for all he believed to be true. He writes, "The Word of God, therefore, is the object and target of faith at which one ought to aim."[6] All Christians then must look to the Bible for all that they need for life and godliness. "We ought surely to seek from Scripture a rule for thinking and speaking. To this yardstick all thoughts of the mind and all words of the mouth must be conformed."[7] But the idea of the Bible's truthfulness was not enough. Calvin and the other Reformers were well aware that those in the Roman Church agreed with them formally on this point.

Where they differed was in the areas of sufficiency and clarity. First, Calvin argued that the Bible in and of itself was *sufficient* as an authority for the church. Why? Because the Church of Rome contended that the Bible was not sufficient for all that the Christian needed for salvation and sanctification. Thus the church councils and customs were needed to establish true religion. On the contrary, Calvin argued that custom and

---

[5]Godfrey, *John Calvin*, 31.
[6]John Calvin, *Institutes, 1536*, trans. F. L. Battles (Atlanta, GA: John Knox, 1975), 58.
[7]Ibid., 62.

tradition, though helpful, were not necessary to establish the authority of the truths of Scripture. The Bible was sufficient.

Second, Calvin spoke about the clarity of Scripture—that the Bible was *clear* as an authority. Rome insisted that the Bible was not only insufficient as an authority but also unclear to the masses. Therefore the church was needed to provide the correct meanings and interpretations. Against this, Calvin stated that the Bible was clear in and of itself to provide the necessary truths that God intended for us to know.

So, for Calvin, as with his fellow Reformers, the idea of Scripture alone as the source of religious truth was a principal element of his final vision for reform. Why is this important?

As heirs of the Reformation, do our churches today have the same confidence in the truthfulness and authority of God's Word? How important is the Word of God for our lives? In many of our churches, the Bible has been functionally rejected in favor of the certainty we hope to gain through rationalism on one side or emotionalism on the other. Our minds or our experiences become the final judge of what is true and right.

Furthermore, do we believe, live, and worship as if the Bible is sufficient? That is, do we take seriously what the Bible has said about what pleases God in our worship, for example? Many seem to think that the Bible is not necessary for things like this. Calvin scholar Robert Godfrey laments,

> The worship of the church has become a feel-good experience, rather than a meeting with the holy God of the universe. Exciting music has become the new sacrament mediating the presence of God and his grace. Sermons have become pop psychology, moralistic exercises in self-help.[8]

We need to hear Calvin's voice once again calling us back to the Scriptures as our only ultimate source of truth and life. In the dedication to his commentary on the general Epistles, Calvin wrote to King Edward of England, "Indeed, if there has ever been a time when the truth of God needed to be freely and boldly maintained, it has never been more necessary than in the present day, as all can see."[9] For Calvin, this required a return to the Scriptures:

---

[8]W. Robert Godfrey, "Calvin and the Need for Reformation"(unpublished manuscript, 2009), 12.
[9]John Calvin, *Calvin's Commentaries: Commentary on First Peter*, trans. W. Johnson (Grand Rapids MI: Eerdmans, 1989), 219.

In case the faithful are carried about by every wind of imposture, in case they should be exposed to the crafty scoffing of the ungodly, let them be taught by the sure experience of faith, and know that nothing is more firm or certain than the teaching of Scripture, and on that support let them confidently rest.[10]

So the first element for his program of reform was the sufficiency and clarity of Scripture to govern our faith and lives.

SOLI DEO GLORIA: THE GLORY OF GOD ALONE

The second element for his program of reform was that which the Scriptures principally taught, namely, that God alone must receive glory as the Savior of his people and the Lord of his church.[11] Confronting a Roman Catholic Church that was pilfering the glory of God, Calvin wrote, "A very great question is at stake: how God's glory may be kept safe on earth, how God's truth may retain its place of honor, how Christ's kingdom may be kept in good repair among us."[12]

Calvin was consumed by a passion for the glory of God. He believed that "once a Christian saw the glory of God as central, then a proper discussion of salvation could follow."[13] This sentiment came out most clearly in his important work *Reply to Sadoleto*. Written in 1539, this essay was a response to a pointed attack against the Reformation by the Roman Catholic bishop Jacopo Sadoleto.

Sadoleto had written the city and church leaders in Geneva urging them to return to the Roman Church. He timed it strategically following the exile from Geneva of Calvin and his fellow reformer William Farel. Not knowing how to respond to Sadoleto, the city leaders contacted Calvin, now stationed in Strasbourg, and requested he respond on their behalf.

One of Calvin's first responses to Sadoleto is especially revealing. Early in his letter, Sadoleto insinuated that Calvin and the other Genevan reformers were motivated by a desire for fame and money. To this, Calvin vehemently responded by saying that what motivated him, above all else, was a concern for the glory of God.[14]

---

[10]Ibid., 225.
[11]Godfrey, "Calvin and the Need," 6.
[12]John Calvin, "Prefatory Address to King Francis I of France," *Institutes of the Christian Religion*, trans. F. L. Battles, ed. J. T. McNeill (Philadelphia: Westminster, 1960), 11.
[13]Godfrey, *John Calvin*, 16.
[14]Ibid.

Sadoleto also had written that the Christian must first be concerned for his own salvation. Calvin, however, maintained that the Christian must first be focused on God and his glory. Calvin wrote,

> It is not very sound theology to confine a man's thoughts so much to himself, and not to set before him, as the prime motive of his existence, zeal to show forth the glory of God. For we are born first of all for God, and not for ourselves.[15]

Calvin argued that the Scriptures principally teach that God alone deserves glory—not only in creation, but especially in his work of redemption. Calvin said that God is glorified preeminently in his breathtaking work of taking unworthy sinners and making them his children through the sacrificial work of his Son.

Calvin believed that God's glory was most tangibly seen in the work of salvation. More specifically, Calvin articulated that a correct understanding of the doctrine of justification was fundamental. Calvin himself had struggled with the consuming question of how to be right with God. In his *Reply to Sadoleto*, Calvin presents his view of the doctrine of justification by faith alone in several steps. To Calvin, there are two steps in justification—two steps for a sinner to become right before a holy God.

First, the sinner comes to recognize his own predicament. Through self-examination, a sinner sees his utter helplessness and hopelessness and the severe judgment required for his sin. This idea of serious soul-searching was central to his theology. Here Calvin not only reiterates a major teaching of the Bible, but also confesses his own personal experience. Throughout the *Reply to Sadoleto*, as well as in his *Institutes*, we find expressions of the very personal struggles with sin and the terrible judgment that awaited him apart from Christ.[16] Calvin knew that seeing oneself in a desperate condition before God was the first step to a sound theology and religious experience.[17]

The second step, after this awareness of hopelessness, is the knowledge of God's way of salvation. He writes, "Then we show that the

---

[15]Calvin and Sadoleto, *Debate*, 58.
[16]For example, he writes, "Every one, therefore, must be so impressed with a consciousness of his own unhappiness as to arrive at some knowledge of God. Thus a sense of our own ignorance, vanity, infirmity, depravity, and corruption, leads us to perceive and acknowledge that in the Lord alone are to be found true wisdom, solid strength, perfect goodness, and unspotted righteousness" (*Institutes*, 1.1.1).
[17]Godfrey, *John Calvin*, 18.

only haven of safety is in the mercy of God, as manifested in Christ, in whom every part of our salvation is complete."[18] For Calvin, the Bible taught the unmistakable truth that Jesus was the Savior who through his sacrificial death fully bore all the sins of his people on the cross, and through his vindicating resurrection credited the saving benefits of his work to them.

How did the sinner receive these promises? Calvin told Sadoleto that faith was the sole instrument by which the sinner received salvation. He stated, "Paul, whenever he attributes to [faith] the power to justifying, restricts it to a gratuitous promise of the divine favor, and keeps it far removed from all respects to works."[19] Faith alone was the instrument to receive salvation.

What was the result? Calvin demonstrated that the result of faith that rests completely on the justifying work of Christ is great peace and assurance for the Christian.[20] In his response to Sadoleto, you can sense the relief and joy in Calvin's words as one whose own burdened conscience found confidence and assurance through faith in Christ.

It is important to note how Calvin finishes his *Reply to Sadoleto* where his response began—with the final authority of Scripture alone. As in his *Institutes*, Calvin argued that the Christian can only find certain authority in the Scriptures. The Bible alone was the heart and life of the Christian community. In fact, Calvin maintained that the church was to honor the Word of God above itself:

> Ours [is] the obedience which, while it disposes us to listen to our elders and superiors, tests all obedience by the Word of God; in fine, ours [is] the Church whose supreme care it is humbly and religiously to venerate the Word of God, and submit to its authority.[21]

For Calvin, then, the Holy Spirit taught the truth of justification through the Scriptures in the church.

In sum, Calvin's *Reply to Sadoleto* revealed the second key element to his program of reform, namely, that God's glory, seen in the salvation of otherwise hopeless sinners, through the work of Jesus culminating at the cross, received by faith alone, was the ultimate goal. God's glory

---

[18]Calvin and Sadoleto, *Debate*, 66.
[19]Ibid., 67.
[20]Godfrey, *John Calvin*, 19.
[21]Calvin and Sadoleto, *Debate*, 75.

fueled Calvin's passion. God's glory motivated Calvin's pen. God's glory brought Calvin peace. And this peace, Calvin knew, could only be known through the Bible. The old church had seriously distorted this truth and was thus in need of thorough reform. One scholar puts it this way: "Theologically the certain church of the Middle Ages was replaced by the certain Scripture of the Reformation."[22]

Calvin's *Reply to Sadoleto* was an important piece of work that solidified the Reformation cause in Geneva. But it was written when Calvin was in Strasbourg. Less than two years after Calvin stayed in Geneva to work with Farel, the city council banished Calvin, Farel, and one other minister from the city over some disagreements.[23]

So Calvin's first exile—from France to Geneva—came to an end with another exile, this time from Geneva. He was twenty-eight years old and probably felt like a failure. After less than twenty-one months, he was rejected as a pastor. His pilgrim life continued. Martin Bucer, the leading Reformer in Strasbourg, invited him to come and help him. He invited Calvin to come pastor a small French refugee community in this German-speaking town. Not knowing what the future held, Calvin the faith-possessed pilgrim continued to trust in his God. Perhaps he was thinking about this time in his life when he wrote, "Whatever kind of tribulation presses upon us, we must ever look to this end: to accustom ourselves to contempt for the present life and to be aroused thereby to meditate upon the future life."[24] He continued to look above, by faith, for his encouragement and hope.

*   *   *

After being rejected by his father at the age of twelve, Kim Gwan Hae and his mother left for Seoul to start a new life—which was extremely difficult, if not impossible, for a single mom at that time. With the help of her siblings, Kim's mother found a place to stay and started to earn a living selling fish.

One year later, in a youth meeting at his friend's church, Kim Gwan Hae was introduced to the gospel of Jesus, and there he committed

[22]Godfrey, *John Calvin*, 22.
[23]Calvin and the other ministers in Geneva disagreed with the city council over who had the ultimate authority in disciplining church members, especially as it related to who could, or, more importantly, could not, participate in the Lord's Supper. See the following for more information regarding this incident: Godfrey, *John Calvin*, 39–42; Selderhuis, *John Calvin*, 75–84; Gordon, *Calvin*, 78–81.
[24]Calvin, *Institutes* (1960), 712.

himself to the Savior. He was so excited about his faith he could not wait to come home and tell his Buddhist mother. Upon telling her, however, Kim was promptly told that if he ever stepped foot in a church again, he would not be welcomed back home. On the following Wednesday evening, he went with his friends to church to attend a Bible study. Upon returning, Kim discovered that the front door was locked. Knock, knock. No answer. Bang, bang! No response. Finally after several minutes, he heard his mother's voice on the other side of the door.

"I told you if you went to church this would no longer be your home." She would not tolerate his desire to be a follower of Christ. Young Kim Gwan Hae had now been banished by both father and mother.

When I asked him how he felt at that time about his new commitment to Christ and the problems it would create, he simply responded that though he did not know much about the Bible, he knew two things: first, that no matter how great a sinner he was, God forgave him in Christ, and second, that no matter what happened in life, God would always be with him. Banished by father and mother, he was a pilgrim displaying faith and hope in God who promised him he would never leave him nor forsake him.

Later in life, he would lead his mother to Christ. He knew in his heart that the only way his mother would come to faith would be for him to demonstrate the grace of God in his words and actions. Allowed to return home shortly after this incident, he began to pray diligently for his mother and also that he would wisely show grace in his words and actions.

Even in the midst of these challenges, Kim Gwan Hae, like Calvin, continued to put his hope in God. Knowing the grace of God in Christ motivated this young Korean to keep looking in faith to the God who had saved him from his sin, for he was a faith-possessed pilgrim who continued to trust and obey.

*   *   *

This leads us to the second stop on our journey. Calvin not only desired to know God more as a student and scholar of the Word of God, but he desired to make him known as a shepherd and servant of the church and world.

MAKING GOD KNOWN: CALVIN THE SHEPHERD
AND SERVANT OF THE CHURCH AND WORLD

As stated earlier, John Calvin was a faith-possessed pilgrim with a singular passion to know God and to make him known. He was keenly aware that one of his main callings in life was to make God known as a shepherd and servant of God. This he did primarily through his pastoral ministry. The bulk of Calvin's pastoral ministry took place in the city of Geneva. During his time in Geneva, Calvin ministered to a community of French Protestant refugees who had fled religious persecution. As one author describes it,

> Calvin's Geneva was comprised of an immigrant population significantly larger than the size of its citizenship. And don't forget, Calvin himself was one—an immigrant who, like the others, wasn't able to vote on civic issues because he was not a native citizen, until near the end of his life. Refugees and immigrants, displaced business people and peasants, royalty and clergy, all of them came to Calvin's Geneva in search of a new life and new possibility. Like us, what they discovered was that new life had to be newly "made-up" in a great experiment: there was no template, no easy answer.[25]

These immigrants—like many immigrants of our day—were trying to restart their lives in the midst of many hardships and challenges. So Calvin, a faith-possessed pilgrim himself, became a shepherd to these fellow pilgrims.

So while he was a pilgrim with a passion for the glory of God, it is important to remember that he used all his gifts, skills, and experiences as a shepherd and servant, ministering what he believed these fellow pilgrims needed. With a foundation in the Word of God, Calvin pastored his flock with great care and compassion through his theology and life, his sermons and letters.

There were two main foundational themes to Calvin's ministry: first, the doctrine of providence and its importance for the Christian life, and second, his theology of worship.

Providence

What drove Calvin as a shepherd? What fueled his ministry? It is important to remember that Calvin, like all of us, struggled with life. He was

[25]Serene Jones, "Calvin and the Continuing Protestant Story," *Modern Reformation* (June/July 2009), 19.

not unaccustomed to suffering. And it is in this context that he contributed such profound teaching on the doctrine of providence.

Fleeing the persecution in Paris, Calvin decided that Strasbourg would be the best place to start his life as a quiet scholar. But God had other plans. Forced to stay one night in Geneva, Calvin encountered the fiery reformer of the city, William Farel, who was so convinced that Calvin needed to stay and join his work, that he pronounced a curse on Calvin should he not stay.

It is here that Calvin took as his personal motto, "My heart I offer to thee, O Lord, promptly and sincerely" and began his pastoral ministry. Though he was exiled from Geneva for a short period near the beginning of his ministry (as we have seen), he faithfully labored in this city for many years.

Much of his training, correcting, rebuking, and comforting of God's people rested in large part on his understanding of providence, that is, God's providential care for his children. Godfrey states, "For Calvin the truth of providence is not simply an abstract or speculative idea about the sovereignty of God but a very practical reality that every Christian needs to understand and embrace."[26] As one who encountered serious suffering himself, Calvin knew that the pilgrims in Geneva had suffered much. In a section entitled, "Without certainty about God's providence life would be unbearable," Calvin wrote the following about this present evil age and its challenges:

> Innumerable are the evils that beset human life; innumerable, too, the deaths that threaten it. We need not go beyond ourselves: since our body is the receptacle of a thousand diseases . . . a man cannot go about unburdened by many forms of his own destruction, and without drawing out a life enveloped, as it were, with death.[27]

Without a clear understanding and hope in God's powerful, personal, and purposeful care over our lives, life and death can only be pointless.

Powerful, Personal, Purposeful

Calvin knew from Scripture that God is all-*powerful* and sovereign. Calvin writes, "[T]ruly God claims, and would have us grant him,

---

[26]Godfrey, *John Calvin*, 140.
[27]Calvin, *Institutes* (1960), 223.

omnipotence—not the empty, idle, and almost unconscious sort that the Sophists imagine, but a watchful, effective, active sort, engaged in ceaseless activity."[28] Calvin argued that nothing happens by chance. All that occurs in our lives and our world is always under the watchful eye and care of our heavenly Father who created and upholds everything by the word of his power (Heb. 1:3).

God is also *personal*. Early in his exposition of providence Calvin uses biblical saints as examples and asks rhetorically, "Whence, I pray you, do they have this never-failing assurance but from knowing that, when the world appears to be aimlessly tumbled about, the Lord is everywhere at work, and from trusting that his work will be for their welfare?"[29] God controls all things personally and actively. He is not some sort of deistic deity, who in creating the world as a clock winds it up and just lets it run its course without his personal and active involvement. This personal character of his providence ultimately comes to fruition in the life, death, and resurrection of the God-man, Jesus. God personally enters time, space, and history to redeem lost sinners for his own glory.

Lastly, God is *purposeful* in his providence. Calvin knew from Scripture that God created this world and is personally involved with it for his own glory and for our good. There was a purpose to creation. Though God created the world for good, mankind fell into sin and received death as a just judgment of this rebellion against his Creator. But God did not leave mankind to this fate. He sent Jesus, his only Son, to live the perfect life that mankind could not live, die sacrificially as a substitute, and be raised to new life as the beginning of a new humanity. From creation and fall to redemption and consummation, God is purposeful in his providential care over his children who put their trust in Christ alone.

Calvin summarizes his thoughts this way: "Gratitude of mind for the favorable outcomes of things, patience in adversity, and also incredible freedom from worry about the future all necessarily follow upon this knowledge."[30] We can live with deep assurance because our sovereign God is our Father, who for the sake of Christ directs all things for our good. Is this not a comforting teaching? It means that not a hair can fall

---

[28]Ibid., 200.
[29]Ibid., 224.
[30]Ibid., 219.

from your head, or a tear from your eye, without your heavenly Father knowing it. Knowing that God is powerful, personal, and purposeful in his care provides much comfort and courage when life is difficult. As pilgrims following a providential God, we can persevere.

Prayer

Calvin encouraged Christian pilgrims to turn to their providential Father and cry out to him in faith-filled prayer. He wrote that when we cry out to God in prayer, God reassures us about his care. He told fellow pilgrims in Christ to remember that God loves them dearly and has purpose for their lives, even (and especially!) in the midst of their challenging circumstances. Calvin devoted pages upon pages to prayer, from his commentary on the Psalms to a large section in his *Institutes*. In fact, his chapter on prayer is longer than his section on predestination.

Calvin believed that the Scriptures, especially the Psalms, teach us to combine prayer with our meditations on the promises and providences of God. Calvin therefore linked the doctrine of providence to prayer, stating that prayer was the way to keep trusting in God even in the most bitter afflictions—be it physical or spiritual. Godfrey writes, "The bitterest afflictions of this life can be sweet when Christians know that they come from God, serve his purposes, and ultimately contribute to their good."[31] As a faith-possessed pilgrim, Calvin had a singular passion to know God and to make him known. One way he did that was to pastor his flock of pilgrims with the comforting doctrine of providence and the prayers that emerge from hearts full of faith and trust in their sovereign God.

Personal Experiences

Calvin was well acquainted with suffering. In 1540, at the age of thirty-one, Calvin married Idelette de Bure, a widow with two children who had joined the Reformed church in Strasbourg that Calvin pastored. Calvin had provided pastoral care to her first husband during his life-ending illness. Less than nine years later, she died. Her health had not been strong, especially after giving birth to Calvin's only child, a son who died only days after birth. They had no other children, though Idelette had several miscarriages. His wife's death struck Calvin deeply. He wrote to a friend,

---

[31] Godfrey, *John Calvin*, 146.

Although the death of my wife has been exceedingly painful to me, yet I subdue my grief as well as I can. . . . I have been bereaved of the best companion of my life, who, if our lot had been harsher, would have been not only the willing sharer of exile and poverty but even of death.[32]

But even in this deep sorrow, he was able to look above.

May [Jesus] support me also under this heavy affliction, which would certainly have overcome me, had not he, who raises up the prostrate, strengthens the weak, and refreshes the weary, stretched forth his hand from heaven to me.[33]

Calvin's own health was never strong. He had regular bouts of malaria-like fever, tuberculosis, ulcerated veins, kidney stones, and hemorrhoids. He identified with the people of God who wrestled with the same problems he did—both physically and spiritually. He poignantly writes about suffering in his commentary on Hebrews 11:1:

Eternal life is promised to us, but it is promised to the dead; we are told of the resurrection of the blessed, but meantime we are involved in corruption; we are declared to be just, and sin dwells within us; we hear that we are blessed, but meantime we are overwhelmed by untold miseries; we are promised an abundance of good things, but we are often hungry and thirsty; God proclaims that He will come to us immediately, but seems deaf to our cries. . . . Faith is therefore rightly called the substance of things which are still the objects of hope.[34]

These words are not just theological statements. They reflected his faith. The struggles of life tested his faith. But at the heart of his faith was the confidence that for the sake of Jesus, God was his loving heavenly Father. So he labored tirelessly pastoring, writing, visiting as only a pilgrim with a singular passion to know God and to make him known could.

We have letters that he wrote to many undergoing suffering—to the sick and grieving as well as to the persecuted. His letters in particular reveal the heart of a pastor that both ached for his brothers and sisters suffering persecution and burned with a passion for God's glory to be manifested through these providential events. And many of the refugees

---

[32]John Calvin, *Selected Works*, ed. J. Beveridge and J. Bonner, vol. 5 (Grand Rapids: Baker, 1983), 216.
[33]Ibid., 219.
[34]John Calvin, *Commentary on Hebrews* (Grand Rapids, MI: Eerdmans, 1974), 157–58.

that he pastored and trained in Geneva would not only become missionaries but martyrs.

His letters sought to build up the faith of those who were experiencing persecution. A key theme that comes up over and over in these letters is where Calvin believed the Christian finds his ultimate source of strength: the grace of God.

But this grace, Calvin said, was received through specific means. Repeatedly in his letters (as well as his other works), Calvin reminded those experiencing persecution and suffering to obtain the grace of God that they needed to endure through prayer and the Scriptures. For through the Scriptures one receives the comfort and encouragement found only in the promises of God.

This leads us to the second great element to his ministry as a shepherd and servant of God's people and world: his thoughts on worship.

Worship

One of the greatest contributions that Calvin made not only in the church in Geneva but to countless other Christians who are heirs to the Reformation is his teaching on worship. Calvin sought to know God and to make him known, and he was convinced that the old church had lost its way regarding worship. Godfrey writes, "He recognized that for most Christians, their experience of God and their knowledge of truth came primarily from worship on Sunday. He wanted to ensure that worship was conducted according to the Word of God."[35]

Why was worship so important to him? For Calvin, corporate worship was the key meeting place of God and his people. This is why in one of his essays entitled "On the Necessity of Reforming the Church," Calvin placed proper worship ahead of the doctrine of salvation on his list of the two most important elements of biblical Christianity.

Calvin approached worship like he approached all things. He would ask, *What does the Bible say?* He held to the principle that the Scriptures must guide public worship so that only what is explicitly commanded in the Bible may be an element of worship. Calvin knew that the human tendency is to think that sincerity and fervor can substitute for truth and faithfulness. He rejected this notion outright.

Further, he was cautious about worship because he knew the heart

---

of man. One of the most profound effects of the fall for Calvin was that men become idolaters. Even among Christians, the temptation to substitute the living God with idols—whatever they may be—remains strong. Therefore, we need to be that much more vigilant in ordering our worship according to the Word of God alone.

Calvin was convinced that through this kind of Scripture-led worship, we receive grace. He argued that the primary means that God uses to bless us is found in the audible Word of God and the visible word of God—the preaching of the gospel and the administration of the sacraments. It is through these preeminent instruments that God chooses to bless and nurture his children. Regarding ministers who spoke for God as they preached, he wrote, "He proves our obedience by a very good test when we hear his ministers speaking just as if he himself spoke."[36]

These are important truths in a day and age when many churches are losing the essence of biblical Christianity. Calvin emphatically did not aim to create "Calvinists." He gave his all to produce biblical Christians. And as he sought to do this, he saw the means of grace at the heart of what the church is to do.

Geneva was filled with gospel-starved refugees and pilgrims yearning to hear the grace of God in the Word of God faithfully preached. Week in and week out, Calvin delivered the Word of God faithfully, expounding the sacred text, giving life-giving water to thirsty souls. But ultimately for Calvin, worship was not a means to an end. Worship was not a means to evangelize or entertain or even educate. Worship was an end in itself. In worship, God meets with his people to bless them.

Calvin was a pilgrim who knew that God was providentially working all things out according to his good and perfect will, so he faithfully continued to pray for grace and to worship God in spirit and in truth.

BURIED IN AN UNMARKED GRAVE

Calvin died peacefully and quietly on May 27, 1564. He was buried in an unmarked grave at a secret location in Geneva. This was his wish—that no one knows where he was buried. He rejected the superstitious veneration of the dead and did not want Christians to make pilgrimages to his grave. Perhaps what he wrote in his *Institutes* serves as a fitting epitaph:

---

[36]Calvin, *Institutes* (1960), 1018.

[W]e may patiently pass through this life with its misery, hunger, cold, contempt, reproaches, and other troubles—content with this one thing: that our King will never leave us destitute, but will provide for our needs until, our warfare ended, we are called to triumph.[37]

Calvin was a faith-possessed pilgrim who had a singular passion to know God (as presented in the Word) and make him known (throughout the world). Calvin was a Christian pilgrim, journeying by faith through the ups and downs of life, with this firm conviction: that by faith in Christ alone he belonged to God, and nothing in this world could ever change that.

*   *   *

Kim Gwan Hae was also a pilgrim who learned about God's sovereign control, providential care, and the experience of grace. Knowing that the only way he could help his mother financially was to get into a good college and then get a good job, Kim studied diligently throughout his junior and senior high school years. He took the national college placement exam, and based on his scores, he received entrance to the most prestigious university in Korea, Seoul National University.

He only received from the University, however, a 50 percent tuition scholarship. Even with the help of his family and friends, he could not afford attending there. So he decided to visit his father—for surely his father would be extremely proud that his first son had received entrance to Seoul National University. He took the train to find his father, and upon seeing him, Kim proudly showed his father the letter of acceptance.

"I came to tell you that your first son got into the most prestigious college in Korea. I hope that brings honor to you and to our family. Since the time I left here six years ago, I have never asked you for anything. I've come today to ask for your help with my tuition."

Kim Gwan Hae waited with anticipation, but almost immediately his father turned to an assistant standing next to him and said, "Tell this young man to leave; I have no son." And so again young Kim Gwan Hae left his father's home stunned, wounded, and empty.

I immediately asked, "Weren't you angry?" Kim turned away and thought pensively.

"Of course I was angry," he said. "Of course I was sad. Of course

---

[37]Ibid., 499.

I was bitter. But what could I do?" He was deeply hurt, but he said that his faith in God's providence kept him going.

Kim Gwan Hae eventually finished college at another university that offered him a full-tuition scholarship. He then emigrated to the United States to attend a graduate school and receive a master's degree in electrical engineering.

Some years later when he received a call from a cousin notifying him that his father was dying, Kim made the trip to see his father one last time. Upon entering his father's bedroom, Kim Gwan Hae spoke tenderly to his father:

"Father, I want you to know why I came today. It's because I'm a changed man. I can honestly say that I love you and I forgive you. I can say that because, even though I didn't have a father, another Father came for me and gave me hope.

"The Bible teaches us that the heavenly Father loved me so much that he sent his only begotten Son Jesus to die on the cross as a sacrifice for my sins. And if you place your trust in him, you too can have your sins forgiven and receive eternal life.

"You never gave me anything in this life, Father. But this is what I want to give you: the opportunity to know this Jesus and put your faith in him."

How could Kim Gwan Hae speak like this? What possessed him? What could so transform this man to love and forgive? Only the grace and glory of God. The grace and glory of God in Jesus had transformed him into a faith-possessed pilgrim with a singular passion of knowing God and making him known—even to those who rejected him. Kim Gwan Hae not only understood God's sovereignty and providence, but he lived it.

Kim eventually would get married and raise a family in the United States, promising himself to give his son a better life, a life of grace, faith, and hope—a life that included the greatest gift of all, the gift of Jesus. How do I know this? Kim Gwan Hae is my father.

However fitting it may be for man seriously to turn his eyes to contemplate God's works, since he has been placed in this most glorious theater to be a spectator of them, it is fitting that he prick up his ears to the Word, the better to profit.

Institutes 1.6.2

If God is for us, who can be against us? He who did not spare his own Son but gave him up for us all, how will he not also with him graciously give us all things? . . . [What] shall separate us from the love of Christ? Shall tribulation, or distress, or persecution, or famine, or nakedness, or danger, or sword? . . . No, in all these things we are more than conquerors through him who loved us. For I am sure that neither death nor life, nor angels nor rulers, nor things present nor things to come, nor powers, nor height nor depth, nor anything else in all creation, will be able to separate us from the love of God in Christ Jesus our Lord.

Romans 8:31b–32, 35, 37–39

2

BAD ACTORS ON A BROKEN STAGE:

Sin and Suffering in Calvin's World & Ours

Mark R. Talbot

The title of this book, *With Calvin in the Theater of God*, came, in part, from the first quotation above. In the *Institutes*, "this most glorious theater" means our universe, and the works referred to are God's work in creation and providence. Like an architect who manifests his greatness in every feature of an opera house from the grand sweep of its tiered balconies to his little touches with its light switches, so God reveals and "daily discloses [his glory] in the whole workmanship of the universe" from the splendor of the heavens to the shape and structure of the toenails on an infant's feet.[1] And just as a human governor may reveal his kindness and mercy and justice in all that he does, so "in administering human society [God] so tempers his providence that, although kindly and beneficent toward all in numberless ways, he still by open and daily indications declares his clemency to the godly and his severity to the wicked and criminal" (1.5.7). And so not only the natural but also the human world is, according to Calvin, "a dazzling theater" of God's glory (1.5.8). In particular, "what are thought to be chance occurrences" in human life are, in fact, Calvin tells us, "just so many proofs of heavenly providence" and "especially of [God's] fatherly kindness" to his children (1.5.8). Yet most people, "immersed in their own errors, are struck blind in such a

---

[1]John Calvin, *Institutes of the Christian Religion* (Louisville: Westminster John Knox Press, 1960), Vol. 1, 52. Hereafter I shall cite the *Institutes* by volume, chapter, and section parenthetically in my text—e.g., for the aforementioned text, "1.5.1." See 1.5.3, 4 and Calvin's commentary on Ps. 139:15 for references to infants and God's skill in forming our toenails and fingernails.

dazzling theater," and so, Calvin stressed, it in fact takes "rare and singular wisdom" to "weigh these works of God wisely" (1.5.8). But if we were to weigh them wisely, then we would see that "there is nothing" in the entire dispensation of human events that God "does not temper in the best way" and that God's glory "shines forth" in all of it (1.5.8).

My task in this chapter is to suggest how we may weigh God's works in ways that allow us to continue believing that God is indeed tempering everything in the best way, even when we become acutely aware of the various kinds and amounts of sin and suffering in our world. How can God's glory be shining forth in all of this?

In the title he chose for this chapter, John Piper pictured all of this sin and suffering in terms of the theater having a broken stage—"The Broken Stage in the Theater of God: Sin and Suffering in Calvin's World." "The idea," John wrote in his invitation to me, "is that even though Calvin saw the world and history as the theater of God, where his glory shone for all to see, he also had a profound view of sin and evil and suffering."

Picturing our world as having a broken stage is illuminating. Because of Adam's and Eve's disobedience, human life until the *eschaton* is always being acted out on a broken stage, a stage strewn with the wreckage of sin and suffering. This makes our acting difficult and sometimes dangerous. We not only find all sorts of obstacles—all sorts of adversities, calamities, and horrors—strewn across the stage's surface, but we also can never be sure that its floorboards are sound and that our feet will not break through as we take our next step, or that the whole surface will not suddenly shift cataclysmically with all of the accompanying damage to us and the overall environment.[2]

Yet here I want to enrich John's metaphor. John wrote that he hoped that my chapter would deal with "some of Calvin's own imperfections, notably the Servetus affair," because he wanted the book's treatment of Calvin to be realistic, and not a whitewash or cheap hagiography. And so let us also picture ourselves as broken. We are all, Calvin included, broken actors on this broken stage. Our first parents' sin has infected us all, and so we are both infirm and untrustworthy, even if we are regener-

---

[2]This is true for the righteous as well as for the unrighteous. As the author of Ecclesiastes puts it,
"[T]he righteous and the wise and their deeds are in the hand of God. Whether it is love or hate, man does not know; both are before him. It is the same for all, since the same event happens to the righteous and the wicked, to the good and the evil, to the clean and the unclean, to him who sacrifices and him who does not sacrifice. As the good one is, so is the sinner. . . . This is an evil in all that is done under the sun, that the same event happens to all" (9:1–3a).

ate. To put this into recent pop-psychology language, each of us carries our own baggage, our own personal and specific weight of damage and sin, and this makes us not only ill-equipped to react well to the difficulties and dangers we encounter on the broken stage, but it also means that our acting may be compromised at any moment by the spiritual, moral, cognitive, and aesthetic evils that tend to spring out of us. We are bad actors, not only in the sense that sometimes we act or react badly, but also in the sense that rather consistently we mean to act badly.[3]

Combined, all of this outer and inner brokenness means that, from our limited human perspectives, our way forward through the world is as uncertain and as prone to result in disaster of one sort or another as when a skier with a bum knee or a bad back is slamming through large moguls. The question is not *whether* he is going to fall; it is just *when*.

GOD'S PROVIDENCE OVER ALL

Calvin declares that "there is nothing" in the entire dispensation of human events that God "does not temper in the best way" and that God's glory "shines forth" in all of it in spite of the fact that Scripture does not gloss over our world's sins and sufferings. In addition to its record of the sin that plunged our world into woe (Genesis 3), Scripture is full of accounts like Rebekah's and Jacob's scheming to cheat Esau out of his blessing (Genesis 27), David's adultery with Bathsheba and his subsequent treachery to Uriah (2 Samuel 11), Gomer's unfaithfulness to Hosea, the Pharisees' plots against our Lord (Matt. 12:14; 22:15–22), and Demas's desertion of Paul (2 Tim. 4:10). It also records events that caused great suffering: wars, famines (Gen. 41:54; 2 Kings 25:3), incest (2 Samuel 13), tornadoes (Job 1:19), and terrible illness.[4] Indeed, it even records some of life's greatest horrors, such as insanity (Mark 5:1–20), suicide (2 Sam. 17:23; Matt. 27:5), infant starvation (Lam. 4:3–4), and even cannibalism (2 Kings 6:24–29; Lam. 4:3–10).[5]

Yet, in the face of all of this, Calvin claimed that God governs nature

---

[3]And so the writer of Ecclesiastes goes right on, after what I have quoted from chapter 9 thus far, to say, "Also, the hearts of the children of man are full of evil, and madness is in their hearts while they live" (9:3b). Of course, this pessimism about human nature carries over into the New Testament in places like Rom. 3:10–18 (which itself quotes and echoes a number of Old Testament passages).

[4]For instance, Job's sickness included festering sores and scabs (7:5; 30:30a), fever (30:30b), excessive thinness (17:7b; 19:20), gaunt, death-like eyes (16:16), and constant, gnawing pain (30:17b). And on top of all of this physical suffering, Job found that his appearance made everyone abhor him (19:13–20; 30:10).

[5]I encourage my readers to keep a Bible close by as they read this chapter to look up the Scriptures cited, since I think that it is crucial that each of us, like the noble Bereans (see Acts 17:11), make sure that all of our theological claims are grounded in God's Word.

and "all [individual] natures" (1.5.6),[6] including human nature and our individual human natures.[7] Because of what he read in Scripture, Calvin was sure that nothing that happens in the natural or human worlds falls out of God's providential hands.[8] In his chapters in the *Institutes* on God's providence, he emphasizes that absolutely nothing in this world comes about—not even a single drop of rain[9]—without God's having willed it.[10] "[N]othing is more absurd," Calvin declares, "than that anything should happen without God's ordaining it" (1.16.8). "*[E]very* success," he insists, "is God's blessing, and [*every*] calamity and adversity his curse" (1.16.8, my emphasis). What "we call a 'chance occurrence'" is simply "that of which the reason and cause are secret" (1.16.8).[11] This does not mean that some events do not appear to us, from our limited

---

[6]E.g., "Concerning inanimate objects we ought to hold that, *although each one has by nature been endowed with its own property, yet it does not exercise its own power except in so far as it is directed by God's ever-present hand.* These are, thus, nothing but instruments to which God continually imparts as much effectiveness as he wills, and according to his own purpose bends and turns them to either one action or another" (1.16.2. my emphasis).

[7]"We do not, with the Stoics, contrive a necessity out of the perpetual connection and intimately related series of causes, which is contained in nature; but we make God the ruler and governor of all things, who in accordance with his wisdom has from the farthest limit of eternity decreed what he was going to do, and now by his might carries out what he has decreed. From this we declare that . . . *the plans and intentions of men, are so governed by his providence that they are borne by it straight to their appointed end*" (1.16.8, my emphasis).

This is not to deny that God often works providentially through intermediary causes: "God's providence . . . is the determinative principle of all things in such a way that sometimes it works through an intermediary, sometimes without an intermediary, sometimes contrary to every intermediary" (1.17.1). Nor should it cut the nerve of human prudence: "The Lord has inspired in men the arts of taking counsel and caution, by which to comply with his providence in the preservation of life itself" (1.17.4). "[T]he Christian heart . . . will ever look to [God] as the principal cause of things, *yet will give attention to the secondary causes in their proper place*" (1.17.6, my emphasis).

[8]"[P]rovidence means not that by which God idly observes from heaven what takes place on earth, but that by which, as keeper of the keys, he governs all events. *Thus it pertains no less to his hands than to his eyes*" (1.16.4, my emphasis).

I think that Calvin is right that Scripture supports such strong claims. Yet space prevents me from rehearsing his arguments for these claims, and so all I am quoting in these footnotes are Calvin's conclusions bereft of their Scriptural support. I would urge those who doubt these claims to work through his arguments in Chapters 16-18 of Book I of the *Institutes*.

[9]"[N]ot one drop of rain falls without God's sure command" (1.16.5).

[10]"God claims, and would have us grant him, omnipotence—not the empty, idle, and almost unconscious sort that [some] imagine, but a watchful, effective, active sort, engaged in ceaseless activity. *Not, indeed, an omnipotence that is only a general principle of confused motion, as if he were to command a river to flow through its once-appointed channels, but one that is directed toward individual and particular motions.* For he is deemed omnipotent, not because he can indeed act, yet sometimes ceases and sits in idleness, or continues by a general impulse that order of nature which he previously appointed; but because, governing heaven and earth by his providence, *he so regulates all things that nothing takes place without his deliberation*" (1.16.3, my emphases).

"[T]hose as much defraud God of his glory as themselves of a most profitable doctrine who confine God's providence to such narrow limits as though he allowed all things by a free course to be borne along according to a universal law of nature" (1.16.3).

[11]"God so attends to the regulation of individual events, and they all so proceed from his set plan, that nothing takes place by chance" (1.16.4).

"[T]here is no erratic power, or action, or motion in creatures, but that they are governed by God's secret plan in such a way that nothing happens except what is knowingly and willingly decreed by him" (1.16.3).

perspectives, as fortuitous (1.16.9), yet "in our hearts it nonetheless [needs to remain] fixed that nothing will take place that the Lord has not previously foreseen" (1.16.9) and that is not "by his wonderful plan adapted to a definite and proper end" (1.16.7).

For many Christians and non-Christians, our world's brokenness means that claims like these wear their falsity on their face. And even for those of us who find Calvin's arguments from Scripture convincing, they may strike us as doubtful if we slam up against something that seems to us to be unacceptably evil. This could be something that has happened in the world—the Rwandan genocide or the babies that starve to death in various parts of the world every day. Or it could be something that has happened to us—the failure of a marriage, a brutal rape, a family member's suicide, or some hideous and yet besetting temptation that we must struggle against each and every day. It could be something biblical—such as God's commanding the Israelites to wipe out whole peoples (Deut. 2:34–35; 7:1–2; 20:16–18). Or it could be something more recently historical—such as the Holocaust. Perhaps it is something big—like the carnage wrought in the destruction of the World Trade Towers. Or perhaps it is something relatively small—like some Christian's seeming inability to control her temper in ways that would allow her to be a much more effective Christian leader who did not leave a slew of hurt people in her wake.

Thinking historically, we may find ourselves questioning Calvin's claims because we hesitate to attribute to God's providence the sorts of ailments and character defects that afflicted, say, Luther and Calvin. Does it seem right to say that God willed Luther's persistent and debilitating rounds of spiritual depression? Ought we to believe that God planned from eternity past Luther's extraordinary and unacceptable crassness—crassness so inappropriate that I dare not even repeat some of it? Again, is it appropriate to lay at God's feet the tragedies, embarrassments, and afflictions that dogged Calvin's life—for instance, the deaths of his infant son and wife; the extreme humiliation of having both his sister-in-law and his step-daughter caught in acts of adultery in his own home; and his constant ill health including migraines, kidney stones (one so large that passing it lacerated his urinary canal), hemorrhoids that at times made it impossible for him to ride or walk and painful for him even to lie in bed, gout, and (particularly debilitating for a preacher and teacher) constant upper-respiratory weakness and distress?

None of this, it would seem, was likely to make Calvin a better leader of the Reformation. And, indeed, in his recent biography of Calvin, Herman Selderhuis writes that "it should come as no surprise that someone who suffered as much illness and pain as Calvin did also had less resistance and patience in other matters, and had a tendency to overreact."[12] And overreact Calvin often did, so much so that Bruce Gordon feels justified opening his new biography of Calvin with these words:

> John Calvin was the greatest Protestant reformer of the sixteenth century, brilliant, visionary and iconic. The superior force of his mind was evident in all that he did. *He was also ruthless, and an outstanding hater.*[13]

Gordon continues,

> Among those things he hated were the Roman church, Anabaptists and those people who, he believed, only faint-heartedly embraced the Gospel and tainted themselves with idolatry. . . . Although not physically imposing, he dominated others and knew how to manipulate relationships. He intimidated, bullied and humiliated, saving some of his worst conduct for his friends.

Some of Gordon's statements are clearly too strong, since among other things, Calvin married a former Anabaptist.[14] Yet, as Selderhuis

---

[12]Herman J. Selderhuis, *John Calvin: A Pilgrim's Life* (Downers Grove: InterVarsity, 2009), 196. Regarding Calvin's ailments, Selderhuis writes:

In the time since his death, Calvin's own descriptions of his maladies have been subjected to medical analysis by specialists. Their findings have suggested that he probably suffered from malaria and tuberculosis, and also had a heart problem or two. All in all, it is a wonder that he reached the age of fifty-five with such a frail body. (200)

[13]Bruce Gordon, *Calvin* (New Haven and London: Yale University Press, 2009), vii, my emphasis. The next quotation is from the same page.

[14]Selderhuis observes that

Calvin did not differ from his fellow Reformers in his *stance* toward [the Anabaptists], but he did in his *approach*, for he thought that [they] had a point when they stressed sanctification of life, imitation, dedication and devotion. They clearly saw the danger of infant baptism, which could be accompanied by the idea that, once baptized, one had made it. They understood that the Spirit not only brought people into communion with Christ but also changed them after his image. There was definitely something to be learned from them, and Calvin was more than ready to do so. He understood why they were bothered by the Reformed. "They are right to take offense, and we give opportunity for it and cannot excuse our damned slowness, which the Lord will not leave unpunished." Calvin's appeal for church discipline also matched well with the Anabaptist insistence on a Christian walk of life and on baptism as a beginning, not an end. He was very engaged with the Anabaptists, and even married an Anabaptist widow, providing a symbol of the way he dealt with them theologically. One had to win them over and bring them into one's own house. In terms of the church, one might even marry them by taking into one's own theological house the good that they bring with them. . . . If today it can notes, "Calvin seems to be aware that even his own character [was] often only another obstacle in his way."[15] I think that, in spite of his repeated efforts to be otherwise, Calvin always was a "difficult personality"—someone who by personality type tended to stand against others, admonishing them, and who was inclined to hew too doggedly to his own way.[16] When we are familiar with a fair amount of Calvin's later life, it becomes dismayingly predictable that, while he was still a schoolboy, he "acquired the [Latin] nickname *accusativus*"—making wordplay on Latin grammar's accusative case—because he was perceived as feeling that he had "a moral obligation to tell on others to the [school] administration."[17]

Yet, Calvin insisted, we learn from Scripture that "there is nothing" in the entire dispensation of human events that God "does not temper in the best way." So why, we may be forgiven for wondering, did God will that Calvin's life and temperament would be this way?

PLACING THE BLAME WHERE IT BELONGS—ON HUMAN BEINGS

This much is certain: in attributing everything that happens ultimately to God's will, Calvin had no interest in shifting the blame. In his *Institutes*, Calvin is very careful to place the blame for human faults where it should be placed—on the propensities and choices of sinful human beings and not on the God who has providentially ordained all things. So far as I know from his writings, Calvin was never tempted, for even a moment, to blame God for his own crankiness, defensiveness, and stubbornness. Calvin knew that insofar as his own character traits involved sin, they were inexcusable and should not persist. He knew that God condemned them and commanded their opposites in Scripture with statements like these:

---

be said that Reformed Christians can learn from their evangelical brothers and sisters, Calvin made the same claim five hundred years earlier. (*John Calvin*, 74)

In mitigation of some of Gordon's other claims, it is also important to remember, as T. H. L. Parker remarks, that Calvin's age demanded polemical invective "as proof of the writer's zeal and sincerity" (T. H. L. Parker, *John Calvin: A Biography* [Louisville and London: Westminster John Knox Press, 2006], 54).

[15] Selderhuis, *John Calvin*, 7–8.

[16] After Geneva's Council of Two Hundred ordered Calvin and the other Reformed ministers to leave the city on the Monday after Easter in 1537, an evangelical synod meeting in Zurich faulted Calvin for "'misplaced vigor' and a lack of tender-heartedness towards 'so undisciplined a people'" (Parker, *John Calvin*, 90).

[17] Selderhuis, *John Calvin*, 14.

The Lord's servant must not be quarrelsome but kind to everyone, able to teach, patiently enduring evil, correcting his opponents with gentleness. (2 Tim. 2:24–25)

Be kind to one another, tenderhearted, forgiving one another, as God in Christ forgave you. (Eph. 4:32)

Put on then, as God's chosen ones, holy and beloved, compassionate hearts, kindness, humility, meekness, and patience, bearing with one another and, if one has a complaint against another, forgiving each other; as the Lord has forgiven you, so you also must forgive. And above all these put on love, which binds everything together in perfect harmony. (Col. 3:12–14)

Calvin's letters show that he took his faults very seriously.[18] In fact, it was part of the Genevan pastors' practice to take each other's faults seriously. T. H. L. Parker highlights this in a passage describing Geneva's Venerable Company of Pastors, which held a regular quarterly meeting "for mutual frank and loving self-criticism":

In the church, as Calvin conceived it, every man helped every other man. If in Christ Jesus all believers are united, then a private believer is a contradiction in terms. Not only are the blessings and the virtues given for the common good, but the faults and the weaknesses concern the other members of the body. There was to be no hypocrisy of pretending to be other than a sinner, no dissembling or cloaking of sins; but, just as God is completely honest with men, and men must be honest with God, so also believer with believer must be courageously honest and open. The quarterly meeting was a little day of judgement when, flattery and convention laid aside, each man saw himself through the eyes of his fellows and, if he were wise, harboured no resentment but knew the uniquely joyful release of voluntary humiliation.[19]

It is unsurprising, then, to find Calvin stating in his *Institutes* that we

---

[18]For instance, Selderhuis writes that in his letters Calvin often mentions
a number of his own negative characteristics of which he was conscious but which he also found difficult to hide. He admitted that it was difficult for him to maintain peace with moderation and tolerance, although he did his best "against his nature." He said that in writing he often became more fiery than he actually intended. . . . When Calvin wrote to Farel that he preferred to live in isolation, part of the reason for this was his realization that his presence could work people up. . . . It would be better for himself as well as for others if he withdrew a little. (*John Calvin*, 30)

[19]Parker, *John Calvin*, 115.

must not lay the blame for our own wickedness upon God, simply because his providence is the "determinative principle of all things" (1.17.2). And thus Calvin explicitly condemns the tendency, as it is sometimes found in the Greek and Roman poets and playwrights, for humans to shift the blame for their own wickedness to God because they take him to be the ultimate cause of what they do.[20] Calvin never doubted that we—and not God—are the instigators of the evil in our acts and thus that we are its cause and we are to blame. "These two statements," Calvin says, "perfectly agree, although in divers ways, that man, while he is acted upon by God, yet at the same time himself acts!" (1.18.2). So rather than shifting everything onto God, Calvin continues, "let [us] inquire and learn from Scripture what is pleasing to God so that [we] may strive toward this under the Spirit's guidance" (1.17.3). We exercise our wills—indeed, we must exercise our wills—and in trying to determine what we are to will, "we must search out God's will through what he declares in his Word," knowing that "God requires of us only what he commands" in Scripture (1.17.5). That much is clear. At the same time, what God providentially wills is part of a "deep abyss" that involves his "incomprehensible plans" that are "hidden from us" (1.17.2). Indeed, we cannot grasp "how God wills to take place [through human wills] what he forbids [in Scripture] to be done" (1.18.3). Yet here we must "recall our mental incapacity, and at

---

[20]Calvin gives three examples, the first from the *Iliad*, where Homer portrays Agamemnon as excusing himself for his quarrel with Achilles during the Trojan war by declaring that it was not he himself who was the cause of his own actions but rather it was "Zeus and fate" (1.17.3; see *Iliad*, Book XIX.74–95). The second and third come from the Roman playwright Plautus (c. 254–184 BC). In the third example, Plautus has a character named Lyconides in his play *Aulularia* excuse himself for the evil he has done on the grounds that the gods willed it. Calvin comments:

> All who will compose themselves in [the proper] moderation will not . . . follow the example of [Lyconides], and cover up their own evil deeds with the name "God." For thus Lyconides says in . . . [a] comedy: "God was the instigator; I believe the gods willed it. For I know if they had not so willed, it would not have happened." (1.17.3)

In my forthcoming book *Unsought Gifts: Christian Suffering*, I work to show that the biblical view of God and his relationship to his creatures is utterly different than the view that we find anywhere else. More specifically, in the biblical materials we don't find the relationship between God's willing something and some creature's willing something to be what is known in economics as a "zero-sum game" in which God's will and his creatures' wills are in competition so that, if God gets his way, then the creature does not (or vice versa). God is not a "super-creature" whose will competes with ours. Rather, God's will is the *sine qua non* of our willing, yet not in such a way that his willing that we shall will something overrides our wills. As the Westminster Confession puts it, "God from all eternity did, by the most wise and holy counsel of his will, freely and unchangeably ordain whatsoever comes to pass: yet so, as thereby neither is God the author of sin, nor is violence offered to the will of the creatures, nor is the liberty or contingency of second causes taken away, but rather established." (2.1)

In two of my articles that are cited in the next footnote, I have argued that it is not possible for us to understand how this can be, although we can understand why we can't understand it. For careful attempts to carry the discussion forward beyond what I have done in those two articles, see Hugh McCann's two pieces "Divine Sovereignty and the Freedom of the Will," *Faith and Philosophy*, Vol. 12, No. 4 (October 1995), 582–98 and "The Author of Sin?" *Faith and Philosophy*, Vol. 22, No. 2 (April 2005), 144–59.

the same time consider that the light in which God dwells is not without reason called unapproachable [1 Tim. 6:16]" (1.18.3).

Calvin admits that understanding why the blame does not run through to God is difficult for "carnal sense," since it "can hardly comprehend how in acting through [evildoers, God] does not contract some defilement from their transgression" (1.18.1). Yet he also asserts that "so great and boundless is his wisdom that he knows right well how to use evil instruments to do good" even though such carnal reasoners, in the fashion of Plautus's Lyconides, "would have transgressors go unpunished, on the ground that their misdeeds are committed solely by God's dispensation" (1.17.5). He then continues,

> I grant more: thieves and murderers and other evildoers are the instruments of divine providence, and the Lord himself uses these to carry out the judgments that he has determined with himself. Yet I deny that they can derive from this any excuse for their evil deeds. (1.17.5)

To try to derive such an excuse would be, he maintains with a neat analogy, as absurd as blaming the sun for the stench of a corpse:

> Whence, I ask you, comes the stench of a corpse, which is both putrefied and laid open by the heat of the sun? All men see that it is stirred up by the sun's rays; yet no one for this reason says that the rays stink. Thus, since the matter and guilt of evil repose in a wicked man, what reason is there to think that God contracts any defilement, if he uses his service for his own purpose? (1.17.5)

Of course, as neat as that analogy is, if you pick at it long enough, it is going to break down, because all of our analogies are drawn from creature-to-creature relations that are different in kind than the Creator-to-creature relation.[21] But Calvin suffers under no illusions here. He is vividly aware that no matter how many neat analogies he deploys, this view of divine providence will always lie open to misunderstanding and misrepresentation. For it is not merely "carnal sense" that cannot comprehend how God's will can be "the truly just cause of all things" (1.16.1).

---

[21]For more on what I am claiming in this paragraph, see my "True Freedom: The Liberty That Scripture Portrays as Worth Having," in John Piper, Justin Taylor, and Paul Helseth, eds., *Beyond the Bounds: Open Theism and the Undermining of Biblical Christianity* (Wheaton: Crossway Books, 2003), 77–109; my "'All the Good That Is Ours in Christ': Seeing God's Gracious Hand in the Hurts That Others Do to Us," in John Piper and Justin Taylor, eds., *Suffering and the Sovereignty of God* (Wheaton: Crossway, 2006), 31–77; and my forthcoming book mentioned in footnote 20.

Comprehending how this can be is simply beyond human mental capacity because no matter how hard or long we try, "we do not"—indeed, I have argued elsewhere, we *cannot*—"grasp how in divers ways [God] wills and does not will something to take place" (1.18.3). Yet in spite of this ever-present danger of misunderstanding and misrepresentation, Calvin will not back away from this claim that God's will is "the truly just cause of all things" because this is what a very close examination of the whole of the Scriptures showed him.[22] In the final analysis, all he can do is to agree with Augustine that "[t]here is a great difference between what is fitting for man to will and what is fitting for God" (see 1.18.3).

WHAT GOOD IS THERE IN SIN AND SUFFERING?

Often, after we have suffered awhile (1 Pet. 5:6–11), the issue of how God in his goodness can providentially will some piece of sin or suffering resolves itself because it becomes clear how he is working for our good through it. For instance, Luther came to recognize that God was being providentially good to him in his times of spiritual depression, as awful as they were. These depressions occurred throughout Luther's lifetime, and it is hard to convey even a rough sense of how harrowing they must have been. "The content of the depressions," Roland Bainton tells us, "was always the same, the loss of faith that God is good and that he is good *to me.*"[23] Luther came to call this experience *Anfechtung*, meaning "all the doubt, turmoil, pang, tremor, panic, despair, desolation, and desperation" that can invade the human spirit. In other words, *Anfechtung* was

---

[22]Calvin believes that biblical history establishes that "God's [eternal] decrees [are not] abrogated" (1.17.14) even in those cases where it seems that "the plan of God does not stand firm and sure, but is subject to change in response to the disposition of things below" (1.17.14). Yet while he believes that this is clear when we think through the cases found in Scripture, he also observes that, in this regard, God "does not express syllable by syllable what is nevertheless easy to understand" (1.17.14).

[23]Roland H. Bainton, *Here I Stand: A Life of Martin Luther* (Nashville: Abingdon Press, 1950), 361. The next quotation in my text is from page 42.

   Bainton notes that Luther's agony regarding these depressions was in his later years "all the more intense because he was [then] a physician of souls; and if the medicine which he had prescribed for himself and for them was actually poison, how frightful was his responsibility" (361). That "medicine" was Luther's whole approach to the Christian life in terms of trusting solely in God's word of mercy as it is found in the Scriptures. And so, as Bainton emphasizes, the Scriptures

   > assumed for Luther an overwhelming importance, not primarily as a source book for antipapal polemic, but as the one ground of certainty. He . . . could not make a beginning from within as did the prophets of the inward word. The core of his quarrel with them was that in moments of despondency he could find nothing within [himself] but utter blackness. (367)

   And thus, on this absolutely crucial point, Luther agrees with our opening quotation from Calvin that no matter how fitting it may be for us to turn our eyes to contemplate God's works, it is even more fitting for us to pay attention to God's Word.

his word for utter hopelessness, for "swarming attacks of doubt" that he
was "irredeemably evil" and consequently that God's love was not for
him, and for his recurrent "grinding sense of being utterly lost."[24] This
would be a terrible experience for any Christian—and it was especially
for Luther as the leader of the Reformation. How could he lead God's
people as his own faith flagged?[25] Yet, as Bainton stresses, Luther became
convinced that without these bouts neither he—nor any other human
being, he thought—could come to "understand Scripture, faith, the fear
or the love of God . . . [or] the meaning of hope."[26] David, he ventured,
"must have been plagued by a very fearful devil. He could not have had
such profound insights if he had not experienced great assaults." As
Bainton observes, this is very close to Luther's saying that

> an excessive emotional sensitivity is a mode of revelation. Those who are
> predisposed to fall into despondency as well as to rise into ecstasy may
> be able to view reality from an angle different from that of ordinary folk.

Bainton continues, "Luther felt that his depressions were necessary.
At the same time they were dreadful and by all means and in every way
to be avoided and overcome." Yet Luther was able to put his struggles
into a context that made spiritual sense of them. And this, ultimately,
made them bearable.[27]

---

[24]James M. Kittelson, *Luther the Reformer* (Minneapolis: Augsburg Publishing House, 1986), 56. After the worst of these *Anfechtung* occurred in 1527, Luther reported to Melanchthon, who was then in Prague, that he had "spent more than a week in death and in hell. My entire body was in pain, and I still tremble. *Completely abandoned by Christ, I labored under the vacillations and storms of desperation and blasphemy against God*" (quoted by Kittelson, 211, my emphasis).

Both Bainton and Kittelson note that it was during the months of this *Anfechtung* that Luther wrote "A Mighty Fortress Is Our God."

[25]In *Luther: An Experiment in Biography* (Garden City: Doubleday & Company, 1980), 307–308, H. G. Haile makes some illuminating comments about how self-doubt played into Luther's depressions. Haile's chapter entitled "*Tentatio Tristitiae*: The Sense of Theology" (*tentatio tristitiae* means the temptation to sadness or despair) expands on the brief remarks in Bainton concerning how Luther became convinced that "the taste of sorrow"—and, more particularly, doubt—was in every way to be resisted and yet, by God's providence, "was the indispensable qualification for a sincere theologian" (304). In fact, Luther credited the development of his entire theology to his struggles: "I did not come to my theology of a sudden, but had to brood ever more deeply. My trials brought me to it, for we do not learn anything except by experience" (quoted in Haile, 304). Indeed, Haile argues that sorrow "as the characteristic lot of man became more and more explicitly central to [Luther's] theology" (302).

[26]Quoted from Bainton, *Here I Stand*, 361. The remaining quotations from and about Luther are from this and the next page.

[27]Bainton opens his chapter on Luther's "Struggle for Faith" by mentioning that when Luther was engaged in allaying the spiritual distress of others, "he drew almost exclusively on that which he had himself discovered to be good [in his own case] for like ailments" (359). This included his helping those who were distressed to realize that "intense upheavals of the spirit are necessary for valid solutions of genuine religious problems. The emotional reactions may be unduly acute, . . . [yet] the way of man with God cannot be tranquil" (361).

Again, while we must not claim to be certain about God's unrevealed purposes in his specific ways of dealing with Calvin, it is not implausible to think that perhaps many of the tragedies and embarrassments and afflictions that dogged his life were intended to teach this immensely brilliant and driven man to rely on God's mercy and providence rather than on his own talents and industry. Through such trials—and even through the sinfulness inherent in his own difficult personality—God may very well have been teaching Calvin that in himself—that is, in his flesh—there dwelt no good thing (see Rom. 7:18).[28]

BUT WHAT IF GOD'S LOVE SEEMS ABSENT?

Yet sometimes, as Calvin puts it, God's "fatherly favor and beneficence" do not "shine forth [for us] in the . . . course of providence," and then "the thought creeps in that human affairs turn and whirl at the blind urge of fortune; or the flesh incites us to contradiction, as if God were making sport of men by throwing them about like balls" (1.17.1). It is then that we are likely to question whether God is indeed tempering everything in the best way.

In these situations, Calvin declares,

> If we had quiet and composed minds ready to learn, [then] the final outcome [of even these situations] would show that God always has the best reason for his plan: either to instruct his own people in patience, or to correct their wicked affections and tame their lust or to subjugate them to self-denial, or to arouse them from sluggishness. (1.17.1)

If our minds were always composed like this so that we could always

---

This doesn't mean that everyone has to have such intense struggles, but it means that even those who don't have them can benefit from the intense spiritual struggles of their fellow Christians. The perspective on reality gained by those who are predisposed to fall into despondency is, as Bainton observes, "a true angle; and when the problem or the religious object has been once so viewed, *others less sensitive will be able to look from a new vantage point and testify that the insight is valid*" (361, my emphasis). Those of us who have suffered intensely often find that God has given us a gift that we can then give to others.
[28]This, as Kittelson (in *Luther the Reformer*) writes, is what Luther saw to be "the deep irony in the Christian life" and thus the very place where Luther found solace:

> Luther found God's grace precisely in the fact and the knowledge of sin. He filled the lectures on Romans with this message: "For God leaves us thus in this sin, in this tinderbox, in self-seeking, so that he may keep us in fear of him and in humility, in order that we may always keep running to his grace, always in fear of sinning, that is, always praying that he not impute it to us and sin begin to dominate." . . . For Luther, the fundamental mystery was this: salvation started from being sinful and knowing it. . . . [And in] those moments when they were most human, most fragile, and most guilty, God was most gracious. "And so sin is left in the spiritual person for the exercise of grace, for the humiliation of pride, and for the repression of presumption" (97).

maintain faith that God as our heavenly Father is good and ceaselessly working for our good, then, no doubt, we would always know what Calvin calls "the immeasurable felicity of the godly mind" (1.17.9). But what happens when something seemingly so awful befalls us that our faith begins to fail? What happens when it seems like anything but God's goodness and glory is what is being made manifest in some instance of sin or suffering—some instance that strikes us as so horrific that we cannot conceive of how it could be part of any "wonderful [divine] plan [that is] adapted to a definite and proper end"?

HORRIFIC SUFFERING

Here, while starting from insights that Calvin gives us, I want to go beyond anything that I am aware that he actually said in order to attempt to give those of us who are struggling, or who may someday struggle, with such situations a way to continue believing that our all-wise, sovereign God is indeed providentially tempering everything for our best.

Now in order to suggest how the "God of all comfort" (2 Cor. 1:3) may be working for his children's good even in the worst imaginable situations, I need to consider an instance of sin and suffering that is so horrific that it appears to make claims like *God is tempering everything in the best way* and *God always has the best reason for his plan* wear their falsity on their faces. So consider this tragedy.[29]

A loving father and husband who has been a conscientious follower of Christ for many years suddenly finds himself beset by a horrific temptation to abuse one of his young children sexually. He struggles mightily against the temptation, repeatedly begging God to take it away. He is, however, so ashamed of what he is struggling with that he cannot bring himself to tell anyone of the horrific desires he is facing.

His struggle continues for years. But then a day comes when he becomes deathly afraid that he is about to succumb. Rather than commit what he recognizes to be a horrific sin, he in his desperation kills himself in a violent and grisly way.

Afterward, his wife and children are left to cope with the enduring pain of having lost a husband and father by means of an act that they can-

---

[29]I am drawing this tragedy together from several situations that I have been acquainted with while changing the details enough that it does not recount any one actual case. Counselors and pastors will know of similar cases, even if they never mention them publicly.

not forget and that they cannot explain. His wife had sensed that he was struggling fiercely with something, and she is left wondering why God did not answer her pleas that he would protect her husband and bring him through whatever was plaguing him. She has always had faith in her heavenly Father and in the efficacy of prayer, but her faith is now gutted, especially as she attempts to reconcile her husband's gruesome death with her prayers that were prompted by our Lord's words:

> Ask, and it will be given to you; seek, and you will find; knock, and it will be opened to you. For everyone who asks receives, and the one who seeks finds, and to the one who knocks it will be opened. Or which one of you, if his son asks him for bread, will give him a stone? Or if he asks for a fish, will give him a serpent? If you then, who are evil, know how to give good gifts to your children, how much more will your Father who is in heaven give good things to those who ask him! (Matt. 7:7–11)

Whenever she recalls these words, she finds herself thinking that no loving earthly father would have willed that one of his children die like this. This blocks her from considering God as a Father for years on end. *If I can't trust these words of Scripture*, she remarks bitterly to just a few of her closest friends, *then what can I trust? How can I believe that God is good in any way?*

Now can anything be said to help someone in a situation like this? How can this woman be encouraged to weigh God's providential work in a way that will allow her to continue believing that God is a loving heavenly Father who is indeed tempering everything in the best way? What hope can we offer her that someday she will see God's goodness and glory shining through this horrible tragedy?

FAITH VERSUS EXPERIENCE

In more pleasant times, our grief-stricken widow would have readily agreed with Calvin that God has made his power, goodness, and wisdom so evident in the design and governance of our universe that even secular poets, "out of a common feeling and, as it were at the dictation of experience," were prompted to call God "the Father of men."[30] She and her husband saw God's handiwork even in the shape and structure of

---

[30]*Institutes* 1.5.3, where Calvin is referring to Paul's quotation from the Stoic poet Aratus in Acts 17:28.

the nails on their newborn baby's feet. But now God's good and gracious Fatherhood is no longer plain.

Her experience is challenging her faith. It does seem to her as if God has made sport of her family by not preventing this horrific turn of events. "But how can I take what has happened," she asks, "in any other way?"

A Place to Start

Perhaps the place to start is with the recognition that our Lord's words in Matthew 7:7–11 do not invite us to evaluate God's Fatherhood according to our ideas of human fatherhood. In quite the opposite manner, our Lord is maintaining that even sinful and ignorant human parenthood gives us some sense of how generous our divine Father must be. For our Lord knew that it is God "from whom all [true] fatherhood descends (Eph. 3:15)."[31]

In other words, the comparison begun in Matthew 7:9 moves, as Calvin notes, "from lesser to greater." And so when we are impressed with great acts of earthly parenthood where we see earthly fathers and mothers forgetting themselves and expending themselves with great generosity upon their sons and daughters, we must remember that they do so only because God "instills a fraction of His own goodness" into them. And thus, rather than allowing our ideas about the virtues of human fatherhood to challenge our faith in God's perfect Fatherhood, we must learn to ask ourselves, "if these little drops have such effect, what may we hope to see from the inexhaustible ocean itself? Or would God be grudging, after thus enlarging the hearts of men?"[32]

---

[31]John Calvin, *A Harmony of the Gospels Matthew, Mark, and Luke* (Grand Rapids, MI: Wm. B. Eerdmans, 1972), 1:230. All of the nonbiblical quotations in this and the next five paragraphs are from this and the next page.

Calvin everywhere stresses that God's Fatherhood is not to be understood by analogy from human fatherhood, but that human fatherhood is only understandable by analogy from divine Fatherhood. So, for instance, he says, in his exposition of the sixth commandment, that "this honor of being called Father properly belongs to God alone and can only apply to men when it pleases him to confer it on them" (in *John Calvin's Sermons on the Ten Commandments* [Grand Rapids: Baker Book House, 1980], 138).

[32]Calvin restates these points arrestingly in his exposition of the Lord's Prayer:

God both calls himself our Father and would have us so address him. By the great sweetness of this name he frees us from all distrust, since no greater feeling of love can be found elsewhere than in the Father. Therefore he could not attest his own boundless love toward us with any surer proof than the fact that we are called "children of God" [1 John 3:1]. But just as he surpasses all men in goodness and mercy, so is his love greater and more excellent than all our parents' love. Hence, though all earthly fathers should divest themselves of all feeling of fatherhood and forsake their children, he will never fail us [cf. Ps. 27:10; Isa. 63:16], since he cannot deny himself [2 Tim. 2:13]. For we have his promise: "If you, although you are evil, know how to give good gifts to your children, how much more will your Father, who is in

This is why our Lord concludes, "If you then, who are evil, know how to give good gifts to your children, how much more will your Father who is in heaven give good things to those who ask him!" (Matt. 7:11). In other words, the still point in our sometimes horrifying world should be our faith that our heavenly Father will never fail to give us good gifts. During life's most disturbing and bewildering moments, we must resolutely remind ourselves that the God who has shown himself to be our heavenly Father in the past will never give us serpents for fish or stones for bread, no matter how snake-like or stone-like one of his gifts may seem.

Sometimes, given our necessarily limited perspectives, the good that God has providentially ordained to come to us through some instance of sin or suffering may be beyond our ken, and then in our prayers we will almost inevitably ask for a lesser gift than the one that God is about to give. Yet this is the very reason, Calvin comments, why our Lord draws this conclusion, for taking Matthew 7:11 to heart can prevent us from giving ourselves too much free rein to indulge in what may prove to be "foolish and unworthy fancies in prayer." And thus, as Calvin rather daringly puts it, Christ subjects our prayers to God's will in order to restrain our Father "from giving us more than He knows is for our good."[33]

We should not, then, "think that [God] has no concern for us when He does not [grant] our requests," for he alone knows what really will temper everything for the best. In fact, we can be sure that our heavenly Father always listens to his children's prayers and that he always responds in what we shall finally know to be a gloriously merciful way, even—and perhaps especially—when it seems that he is not listening or doesn't care about what informs our most desperate pleas, for as the author of

---

heaven" [Matt. 7:11]? Similarly, in the prophet: "Can a woman forget her . . . children? . . . Even if she forgets, yet I shall not forget you" [Isa. 49:15]. (3.20.36)

[33]In the *Enchiridion*, Augustine helpfully observes:

Now sometimes with a good will a man wishes something which God does not wish, though God's will is also good (evil it can never be) and much more fully and more surely good. For example, a good son wishes his father to live, whom God with a good will wishes to die. And, on the other hand, it can happen that man with a bad will wishes something which God wishes with a good will—for example, if a bad son wishes his father to die and this is also the will of God. To be sure, the good son wishes what God does not wish, while the bad son wishes that which God also wishes, yet the piety of the one, even though his wish is contrary to God's, is more in accordance with the good will of God than the impiety of the other, though his wish is the same as God's. *There is a great difference between what is proper for a man to will and what is proper for God, and to what end each man applies his wish*; on this difference depends the approval or disapproval of the wish. For God accomplishes some of His purposes, surely good ones, through the evil wills of evil men. (Augustine, *Faith, Hope and Charity* [Washington, DC: The Catholic University of America Press, 1947], 454–55 [chapter 26, section 101], my emphasis)

Lamentations reminds us, while our God may cause us grief, yet "he will have compassion according to the abundance of his steadfast love; *for he does not willingly afflict or grieve the children of men*" (Lam. 3:32–33, my emphasis).

Still, since our emotions often shape our prayers and "all our emotions are blind, we must seek [our] pattern of prayer" not primarily from what our hearts often desperately want but "from [God's] Word." And this means that anyone who "wishes to approach God with confidence in his prayer, should learn to curb his heart, and ask for nothing which is not in accordance with His will," as several biblical passages suggest (James 4:3, 13–17; Matt. 6:10; Luke 22:42).

Perfect Parenting

In the abstract, it should not be hard for any Christian to acknowledge truths like these. Indeed, it doesn't take faith to recognize how sensible this general perspective is.

Virtually everyone will concede, for instance, that even earthly parents are justified in not granting their children's pleas if they know that to grant them would mean that their children would thereby forgo some greater good. Indeed, they would not be good parents if they granted such pleas, for part of their parental role is to seek goods for their children that lie further out than their children can currently see. The little girl who pleads with her daddy to cancel the upcoming surgery that she is dreading so much must not prevail if she is to gain through that surgery a good beyond what she can presently conceive.

We know, as well, that children's emotions tend to get away from them, sometimes making them want what they should not have and sometimes making what are very good gifts seem like mere stones or snakes. The boy who wants the same kind of shoes as "everybody else has" in order to feel as if he is cool is not likely to appreciate getting what is actually a better make.

Yet the horror of her tragedy eclipses these truths for our widow. In the throes of her suffering, she cannot conceive of any good that could be so great that it would justify God's having ordained this tragedy.

Ordinarily, Calvin points out, we deliberately suspend making negative judgments about others "rather than be charged with rashness" for being more certain about their intentions and actions than we have any right to be (1.17.1). In other words, we readily moderate our judgments about what other human beings are intending or doing, often also acknowledging that they are not required to render an account of themselves to us. Yet, Calvin observes, we "haughtily revile the hidden judgments of God, which"—much more than with the unknown and often inappropriate intentions and actions of our fellow human beings—"we ought to hold in reverence" (1.17.1). And we do this, Calvin reminds us, even though Scripture explicitly states "that [God's] judgments are a deep abyss" (1.17.2; see Eccl. 3:10–11; 8:16–17).

SCRIPTURE PLUS EXPERIENCE

This means, Calvin concludes, that "no one will weigh God's providence properly and profitably but him who considers that his business is with his Maker and the Framer of the universe, and with becoming humility submits himself to fear and reverence" (1.17.2). God has not promised that his children will be free of either sin or suffering.[34] And, consequently, acknowledging that every aspect of our lives is subject to his providential sovereignty (Ps. 139:16) means that it is not inappropriate for God's children to feel reverent fear at what he may have ordained for them (Luke 12:4–7). For although it will ultimately be undeniably clear to us that God never does anything that is wrong (Deut. 32:4; Dan. 4:34–37; Rom. 3:4–6; Rev. 15:2–4),[35] we cannot know what he has in store for us (James 4:13–16), and Scripture reveals that he sometimes ordains fearsome things (Ruth 1, esp. vv. 13, 20–21; Job 1:20–22; 2:9–10; Ps. 88:6–8, 14–18).

So, we may ask, how can we remain assured that God "will not suffer anything to happen [to us] but what may turn out to [our] good and salvation" (1.17.6)? When bad things happen to us, are there ways to stop feeling that we have been given serpents for fish and stones for bread?

In these situations, we need to know, Calvin writes, the Bible's promises that "God's singular providence watches over the welfare of believers"[36] as well as to become acquainted with Scripture's examples of

---

[34]See footnotes 2 and 3.
[35]Calvin says that God's "providence . . . [is] that determinative principle of all things, *from which flows nothing but right*, although the reasons have been"—at least for now—"hidden from us" (1.17.2, my emphasis).
[36]See his enumeration of some of these promises at 1.17.6.

God's "great diligence" in caring for his saints.[37] We also need to trust the biblical testimonies that "teach that all men are under his power, whether their minds are to be conciliated, or their malice to be restrained," so that either their malice does us no harm (1.17.7) or its harm is only such as is "permitted or sent by God's just dispensation" (1.17.8). "Gratitude of mind for the favorable outcome of things, patience in adversity, and also incredible freedom from worry about the future" all necessarily follow, Calvin declares, when we believe these biblical verities.[38]

Yet it is through actual suffering that our knowledge of these verities goes from being merely abstract to become concrete:

> We rejoice in our sufferings, knowing that suffering produces endurance, and endurance produces character, and character produces hope, and hope does not put us to shame, because God's love has been poured into our hearts through the Holy Spirit who has been given to us. (Rom. 5:3–5)[39]

> Count it all joy, my brothers, when you meet trials of various kinds, for you know that the testing of your faith produces steadfastness. And let steadfastness have its full effect, that you may be perfect and complete, lacking in nothing. (James 1:2–4)

Sensing God's love when we are in the midst of situations where human affairs seem to turn and whirl at the blind urge of fortune assures us "that God's singular providence is still keeping watch to preserve [us], and will not suffer anything to happen but what may turn out to

---

[37]See 1.17.6, where Calvin claims that "the principal purpose of Biblical history is to teach that the Lord watches over the ways of the saints with such great diligence that they do not even stumble over a stone [cf. Ps. 91:12]." Of course, this statement must be interpreted as carefully as our Lord's statements in Matthew 7:7–11. Its truth for Christians is rooted in the perspective given in passages like Romans 8:18—"I consider that the sufferings of this present time are not worth comparing with the glory that is to be revealed to us"—and 2 Corinthians 4:17—"this light momentary affliction is preparing for us an eternal weight of glory beyond all comparison." In other words, the sorts of statements made in Psalm 91—e.g., "no evil shall be allowed to befall you, no plague come near your tent. For he will command his angels concerning you to guard you in all your ways. On their hands they will bear you up, lest you strike your foot against a stone"—are not to be taken as promises that God will keep us from all evil in this life but as promises that, no matter what evil we face here, we shall ultimately count it as nothing compared with the joy that we shall know forever in Christ.

[38]1.17.7. Calvin's exposition about raising our hearts to God when we suffer mistreatment at the hands of other human beings is not to be missed; see the first paragraph of 1.17.8.

[39]Paul articulates another good that comes from suffering in 2 Cor. 1:3–4, where he says that the God of all comfort, "comforts us in all our affliction, so that we may be able to comfort those who are in any affliction, with the comfort with which we ourselves are comforted." A couple of verses later he tells the Corinthians that they "experience" comfort when they patiently endure the same sufferings that he and Timothy suffer. And this makes Paul hopeful for them.

[our] good and salvation,"[40] and having the opportunity sometimes to recognize the final, providentially ordered outcome in situations where it seemed that God was making sport of us goes a long way toward assuring us that he "always has the best reason for his plan." And thus it is primarily in and through our encounters with this world's sin and suffering that we begin to enjoy "the immeasurable felicity of the godly mind."

Paul's Stake

Whenever I have been in the throes of suffering, I have found it crucial to remind myself that Paul's words in Romans 5 were forged in his own suffering. In 2 Corinthians 11:16–12:10, he chronicles part of what it meant for him to have been called to suffer for Christ's name (Acts 9:16): he had endured three (indeed, later four) shipwrecks that included a night and a day adrift at sea; he had been repeatedly imprisoned and five times lashed and three times beaten with rods as well as once stoned; he had been in danger from rivers and robbers as well as from Jews and Gentiles and false Christians; he had known many cold and sleepless nights and hungry and thirsty days; and he was in constant anxiety for all of the churches.

Expanding just one of Paul's claims disabuses us of any tendency to dismiss the depths of his sufferings by thinking that ours must be worse.[41] "Five times," he writes, "I received at the hands of the Jews the forty lashes less one" (2 Cor. 11:24). This punishment, Paul Barnett comments,

> arose from Deut. 25:1–5. . . . In no case was the beating to exceed forty [lashes], administered to the man or woman bending down. . . . The minister of the synagogue was to stand on a raised stone inflicting the blows "with all his might," using a redoubled calf strap, to which two other straps were attached. Thirteen blows were delivered to the chest and twenty-six to the back.

---

[40]Moo says that the sequence of "linked virtues" that we are given in Romans 5:3–5 is one that our suffering inaugurates and that ends in an "inner, subjective certainty that God does love us." This love, he says, "is conveyed to our sensations by the Holy Spirit, who resides in every believer," and "it is this internal, subjective—yes, and even emotional—sensation within the believer that God does indeed love us—love expressed and made vital in real, concrete actions on our behalf—that gives to us the assurance that 'hope will not disappoint us'" (Douglas J. Moo, *The Epistle to the Romans* [Grand Rapids, MI: William B. Eerdmans, 1996], 303–305).

[41]Through his pastoral work of counseling others, Luther came to the conviction in his later life that "sorrow [was] the essence of human existence," even though early on, Haile notes, he thought that his own experiences of suffering "were singular, if not unique." Later, however, he "recognized one of [suffering's] great dangers [was] the self-centered belief that 'No one is suffering like me'" (H. G. Haile, "Tentatio Tristitae," in *Luther: An Experiment in Biography,* [Garden City, NY: Doubleday & Company, 1980], 301).

"The severity of this beating," Barnett observes, "can be inferred from the provisions made in the event the offender defecated, urinated, or even died as a result of the blows."[42]

At the end of this partial chronicle of his sufferings—most of which had become such a "normal" part of the apostle's life that they are not even mentioned elsewhere in the New Testament[43]—Paul mentions the "thorn in his flesh" that God had given him, "a messenger of Satan" that God meant to torment him (2 Cor. 12:7). The Greek word for this thorn is *skolops*, which means a thorn or a stake; and so the idea conveyed by this verse is that God had "gifted" Paul with this *skolops*, which was constantly pricking him or "staking him down" to keep him from becoming "over-lifted" or made conceited by the revelations he had heard and seen.

"God," Barnett says, "brought [Paul] down to earth by his *skolops*, and kept him there, buffeting him" day by day.[44] Three times, Paul tells us, he pleaded with the Lord to take this *skolops* away (12:8). But our Lord would not remove it, saying to Paul, "My grace is sufficient for you, for my power is made perfect in weakness" (12:9). And so, for Christ's sake, Paul concludes, "I am content with weaknesses, insults, hardships, persecutions, and calamities. *For when I am weak, then I am strong*" (12:10, my emphasis). "Meekness, gentleness, humility, patience, and endurance—the Christlike marks of an apostle, of which [Paul] has much to say in this letter—are," Barnett observes, "connected with God's 'gift' to him of the *skolops*." Paul's constant suffering staked him down to the reality of his own weakness in a way that meant he knew that he could not survive without constantly relying on God's grace and mercy.

---

[42]Paul Barnett, *The Second Epistle to the Corinthians* (Grand Rapids, MI: William B. Eerdmans, 1997), 542.

[43]For instance, as Barnett notes, "the famous shipwreck en route to Rome (Acts 27:12–44) occurred subsequent to the writing of 2 Corinthians" (ibid., 543)—and so we have no other record of the three shipwrecks mentioned in 2 Corinthians, as stressful as they must have been.

[44]Ibid., 568. My next quotation from Barnett is from the same page.

In his comments on this verse, Calvin remarks that for Paul to describe himself as "buffeted" by his stake or thorn is "a most eloquent way of indicating that he was brought back into order"—or, in other words, kept properly humble. He continues:

> To be buffeted is a severe indignity. If anyone's face is beaten black and blue, shame prevents him from showing himself to others, and so when we labour under any kind of infirmity, we should remember that we are, as it were, being buffeted by the Lord to make us ashamed, so that we may learn humility. This should be borne in mind especially by those who are outstanding for their distinguished excellencies, for if they have defects mixed with their virtues . . . these are not merely the rods of their heavenly instructor but the buffetings which are designed to restrain all haughtiness and fill them with modesty. (*The Second Epistle of Paul the Apostle to the Corinthians and the Epistles to Timothy, Titus and Philemon* [Grand Rapids, MI: Wm. B. Eerdmans, 1964], 159)

A few sentences later, Calvin encourages us to remember who is saying this: it is the apostle Paul, who had overcome all sorts of "torments and perils and other evils," and yet "there still went on in him a conflict so doubtful that he could not conquer without being buffeted" (160).

Suffering and Glory

Our grief-stricken widow feels herself staked down and buffeted day by day. As she ponders the horrific finality with which her husband's life ended, she cannot imagine any future state that could be so good that it would reconcile her to this awful tragedy. For her, right now, there simply seems to be no way that this tragedy could possess a final outcome that could lead her to confess that God has had the best reason for his plan.

Yet if the faith that she has believed is true, then there really are goods to which she, as one of God's children, shall someday be heir that are right now beyond even her wildest imaginings. And, Paul claims, these goods will be so glorious that her current sufferings will not be worth comparing with them (Rom. 8:18).

Indeed, what in fact awaits her in the *eschaton*—in the final, blessed state after our Lord has returned, when God will be with us, having wiped every tear from our eyes, and when there shall be no more death or mourning or crying or pain (Rev. 21:3–4)—is an "eternal weight of glory" that is literally incommensurable[45] with what Paul dares to call the "light momentary affliction" that she is now undergoing (2 Cor. 4:17).[46] Right now, of course, it is virtually impossible for her to conceive of a future good that could be so great that it will make her suffering seem "light" and "momentary."[47] Yet this inconceivability is exactly what she should expect, because the incommensurably great eschatological good that awaits her is something that no human eye can naturally see nor any human ear can naturally hear nor any human heart can naturally imagine (1 Cor. 2:9). Indeed, its glories are "utterly beyond description."[48] And this is the good that

---

[45]That is, not even comparable, "beyond all comparison" (2 Cor. 4:17).

[46]Paul frames the truth of 2 Corinthians 4:17 in the first-person plural, meaning it to cover all believers, including himself (see Barnett, *Second Epistle to the Corinthians*, 253). And so his declaration that all of our affliction now is just "light" and "momentary" is not meant to be dismissive of the way that our widow's or anyone else's suffering currently feels, since he opens 2 Corinthians by confessing that he underwent suffering in Asia that was so great that he and whoever was with him were "so utterly burdened beyond our strength that we despaired of life itself. Indeed, we felt that we had received the sentence of death" (1:8–9). As Barnett comments on 4:17, Paul's contrasting the momentary, light suffering that we experience now with the eternal weight of glory that we shall know in the *eschaton* is not a matter of him minimizing "the pain of suffering. Rather, it is a matter of perspective. Suffering, real though it is, is ephemeral because it belongs to this age, in contrast with the age to come, which is eternal" (252).

[47]While commenting on Romans 8:18, Moo says (in *Epistle to the Romans*), "We must, Paul suggests, weigh suffering in the balance with the glory that is the final state of every believer; and so 'weighty,' so transcendently wonderful, is this glory that suffering flies in the air as if it had no weight at all" (511). He then quotes 2 Corinthians 4:17.

[48]The *New International Version*, which is the basis of Barnett's commentary series, translates 2 Corinthians 4:17 like this: "For our light and momentary troubles are achieving for us an eternal glory that far outweighs them all," but Barnett then in effect corrects the appearance of commensurability

God has prepared "from the foundation of the world" (Matt. 25:34; cf. Eph. 1:4; Rev. 13:8) for our widow and her family insofar as they are among those who love him (see 1 Cor. 2:9 with Rom. 8:28). In other words, it is what our Father has always had in mind for her and her family, even though it lies much further out than she, as his child, can currently see.

As we should expect with a God who is a perfect Father and who does not "willingly afflict or grieve the children of men," the links between her suffering and her glorification are not accidental. In fact, the New Testament inextricably links the future eschatological goods that await us with our present temporal suffering (see, e.g., Mark 10:28–30; John 15:18–20; Acts 14:19–23; Rom. 8:16–17; 2 Cor. 1:7). As Paul puts it, we suffer with Christ "*in order that* we may also be glorified with him" (Rom. 8:17). "The suffering," Barnett notes, "'prepares' the glory 'for us,'"[49] in the sense that "under [God's] loving hand every evil thing works together for the good—that is, the *end-time* good—of those who love him. Only those who have no genuine vision of eternity," he adds, "think otherwise." But, of course, if this is so, then God must not cancel our sufferings, no matter how hard we plead.[50]

Yet to say that our suffering prepares the glory for us is only part of Paul's thought in 2 Corinthians 4:16–18, the whole of which reads,

---

between the troubles and the glory by commenting that the "eternal weight of glory . . . is 'utterly beyond description'" (252).

The same temporal/eternal contrast occurs in 1 Peter—"Humble yourselves, therefore, under the mighty hand of God so that at the proper time he may exalt you, casting all your anxieties on him, because he cares for you. . . . And after you have suffered *a little while*, the God of all grace, who has called you to his *eternal glory* in Christ, will himself restore, confirm, strengthen, and establish you" (5:6–7, 10, my emphasis)—and the same inconceivability of the state of glory in 1 John—"Beloved, we are God's children now, and *what we will be has not yet appeared*; but we know that when he appears we shall be like him, because we shall see him as he is" (3:2, my emphasis).

[49]See Barnett on the Greek verb *katergazomai*, which, he comments, "implies a long process, a 'working out'" (252,n18). *Katergazomai* is the verb that appears in the syllogistic chains regarding suffering that are found in Rom. 5:3–5 and James 1:2–4, although in those places the process is one that finds its completion in this life.

The following quotations in my text are from 252–53.

[50]In commenting on the last phrase of Romans 8:16–17—"The Spirit himself bears witness with our spirit that we are children of God, and if children, then heirs—heirs of God and fellow heirs with Christ, *provided we suffer with him in order that we may also be glorified with him*"—Moo says:

[I]n a typical NT preservation of the "eschatological reservation," Paul adds that this glorious inheritance is attained only through suffering. . . . Paul makes clear that this suffering is the condition for the inheritance; we will be "glorified with" Christ (only) *if* we "suffer with him." Participation in Christ's glory can come only through participation in his suffering. What Paul is doing is setting forth an unbreakable "law of the kingdom" according to which glory can come only by way of suffering. . . . Just as, then, Christ has suffered and entered into his glory (1 Pet. 1:11), so Christians, "fellow heirs with Christ," suffer during this present time in order to join Christ in glory. (505–506)

So we do not lose heart. Though our outer self is wasting away, our inner self is being renewed day by day. For this light momentary affliction is preparing for us an eternal weight of glory beyond all comparison, as we look not to the things that are seen but to the things that are unseen. For the things that are seen are transient, but the things that are unseen are eternal.

The crucial clause here is found right at the beginning of verse 18— namely, "*as* we look not to the things that are seen but to the things that are unseen." Barnett notes that this participial construction "carries the idea '*since* we do not look at,' or even '*provided* we do not look at,'" which means it needs to be read as qualifying the way in which "this light momentary affliction is preparing for us an eternal weight of glory" in verse 17.[51] So, Barnett concludes, the "'preparation for us' of an 'eternal weight of glory' in the coming age does not occur by a merely mechanical process through our 'suffering' in this age." Our suffering alone does not prepare for us the glory. "Rather," Barnett says, the "'suffering' of this age 'prepares . . . glory . . . for us,' *provided* 'we do not look to the things that are seen but to the things that are not seen.'" It is what we are thinking about as we are suffering that affects whether that suffering is preparing an eschatological weight of glory for us. More specifically, we must not be thinking about this-worldly, transient things but about eschatological, eternal things.[52]

Likewise, Barnett notes, the same qualification needs to be applied to the day-by-day renewal of our inner selves that is mentioned in verse 16. Our inner self is renewed, even as our outer self is wasting away in grief or other kinds of suffering, as—and *only* as—"the believer looks to things as yet unseen."

So our grief-stricken widow's current suffering is preparing for her an incommensurably great eschatological glory, provided she does not

[51]Ibid., 254, my emphasis. If Barnett is right about how this participial clause should be construed, then perhaps the best recent translation of vv. 17–18 is the Revised Standard Version, which reads: "For this slight momentary affliction is preparing for us an eternal weight of glory beyond all comparison, *because* we look not to the things that are seen but to the things that are unseen; for the things that are seen are transient, but the things that are unseen are eternal."

My next two quotations from Barnett are from the same page, and my final quotation, at the end of my next paragraph, comes from the previous page. Barnett points out that the "is being renewed" of v. 16 is "in the passive voice [and thus] indicates that God is responsible for that process" (254).

[52]Barnett's exposition needs a little qualification, since there are situations—such as a Christian's committing suicide while in a state of desperation or despair—where God as that Christian's Father will still bring him or her through to glory because of the atoning work of Christ and in spite of the fact that the person did not persist in "looking . . . to the things that are unseen." Paul's words are not meant to limit the degree to which our Father may show us mercy and grace in spite of our failings.

focus on the horrors with which her husband's earthly life ended but, rather, fixes her gaze on the glorious hope of what is still to come for him and for her and for their family. And it is as she does this that God will re-create her inner self even while, in her perfectly justified grief, her outer self wastes away.[53]

WITH EAGER LONGING

"Yet what," our widow may justifiably ask, "is this glorious hope that I am to fix my gaze upon? Are you forgetting that the worst thing about this whole tragedy is that it strikes me as so horrific that I cannot imagine how any future state could be good enough for me to confess that God has been acting as our perfect heavenly Father in ordaining it?"

No, I haven't forgotten this. But I am trying to help our widow to realize that God as a perfect heavenly Father is always more concerned with the great eternal eschatological glory that he has ordained for us than with the merely transient earthly goods and evils that prepare that glory for us. Once we have experienced that final glory, it will be perfectly clear that through all of life's earthly joys and sorrows our Father has indeed always been tempering everything for our best.

The enormity of her tragedy is what makes keeping this glorious hope in mind so difficult for our widow to do. But here, as 2 Corinthians 4:16–18 emphasizes, she has a clear choice to make: Either she can let this tragedy falsify her long-held belief in God's perfect Fatherhood, or she can deliberately suspend making that negative judgment because she realizes how limited her earthly perspective necessarily is and how blind her current emotions may be.

When we recall what virtually everyone concedes about human parents and children, it is clear, at the very least, that letting this tragedy falsify her long-held belief is certainly no more rational than deliberately suspending that negative judgment.

In fact, I think that we can go one more step toward helping her fix her gaze on the glorious hope by saying a bit more about what awaits those who believe.

---

[53]My conclusion here just rephrases, in the third-person singular, this paragraph of Barnett's:
> Thus, we do not focus on the present time, including the suffering and disappointment. Rather, we fix our gaze—metaphorically speaking—on the glorious hope that will be realized in the age to come. As we do so, God will re-create our "inner person," even though our "outer person" is decaying. (254)

One More Step

From eternity past, it has been God the Father's plan to glorify his Son by gathering a bride for him from among all the earth's nations (Eph. 1:3–14; Rev. 21:2, 9; cf. John 3:29). Our Lord, God's Lamb, has purchased this bride for himself with his own blood (Rev. 5:9) by becoming a curse for her (Gal. 3:13) and dying in her place (John 11:50–52; Eph. 5:2, 25). And thus he has saved her (Rom. 5:1–2, 6–11) and is sanctifying her (Eph. 5:26) so that "he might present [her] to himself in splendor, without spot or wrinkle or any such thing, that she might be holy and without blemish" (Eph. 5:27; cf. 2 Cor. 11:2).

In the *eschaton*, our Lord, as the Bridegroom, will lead us, his bride, "into the romance of eternal salvation."[54] And we, as his bride, shall then "forget our people and our father's house"—think of our current joys and sufferings, which will not be worth comparing with the glory that shall then be—and "with joy and gladness be led along as we enter the palace of our God and King."[55] And he "will desire the beauty" that he has wrought in us, and we shall become one with him (Eph. 5:29–32).

The Old Testament's bridal imagery, David Aune observes, "primarily emphasizes devotion (Jer. 2:2) and the joy of the bride (Isa. 61:10; 62:5); *the voice of the bridegroom and the bride were proverbial for mirth and gladness* (cf. Jer. 7:34; 16:9; 25:10; 33:11)." This imagery gives our Lord's parables in Matthew 22:2–14 and Matthew 25:1–13 their punch, and it forms the basis of the great eschatological consummation as it is represented in Revelation 21:1–2, 9–11, and 22:17. And, as we find in the Old Testament's greatest expression of romantic love (see the Song of Songs), the inexhaustible wonders of our life in Christ will thenceforth and forevermore be best expressed in song—in what both Testaments describe as a new song, a song of praise for our salvation (see Rev. 5:9–10; Ps. 33:1–3; 96:1–6; Isa. 42:10–12) that will celebrate how

---

[54]See the *ESV Study Bible*'s note on Isaiah 61:10, which reads, "I will greatly rejoice in the LORD; my soul shall exult in my God, for he has clothed me with the garments of salvation; he has covered me with the robe of righteousness, as a bridegroom decks himself like a priest with a beautiful headdress, and as a bride adorns herself with her jewels."

[55]My quotation marks in this sentence and the next demarcate images that I am adapting from Ps. 45 (especially vv. 6, 10, 11, 15), which is a love song celebrating a royal wedding. As David Aune observes, "While it is technically correct to claim that the allegory of the bridegroom (=Yahweh) was never applied to the Messiah by Judaism . . . the messianic interpretation of the Royal Wedding Song preserved in Ps. 45 . . . saw the Messiah in the figure of the king-bridegroom," the New Testament applies some of the statements made in that psalm to Christ (David E. Aune, in *The International Standard Bible Encyclopedia*, revised edition [Grand Rapids, MI: William B. Eerdmans, 1979], 1:1, 546). My next quotation from Aune (to which I have added the emphasis) is from the same page.

our Lord has ransomed us from futile ways (1 Pet. 1:18) and has shown us the path of life (Ps. 16:11). Apart from him, we shall sing, we have no good (Ps. 16:2); he alone is our chosen portion (Ps. 16:5), and in his presence is found the fullness of joy (Ps. 16:11).

Our Own Song to Sing

Now in this eschatological state, each of us will have his or her own song to sing—a song of how our God and Savior has wrought our individual salvation and has been particularly providentially merciful to us,[56] planning all of the details of our lives from before our births (Ps. 139, especially vv. 13–16), and watching over us so carefully that even the very hairs of our heads are numbered (Matt. 10:30) so that even if we go through great suffering, not one of those hairs will perish (cf. Luke 21:10–18). There, if indeed he is numbered among God's children, our widow will find her husband singing of the wonders of his salvation and of the inexhaustibly merciful way that God has dealt with him in spite of and indeed even because of his sin.[57] He will be singing of the redemptive love of his Savior who died for him while he was still weak and indeed dead in his trespasses and sins (Rom. 5:6–11; Eph. 2:1–7). And his song—in a particularly poignant and powerful way that will be inextricably linked with the suffering that his horrific temptation gave to him as well as his final, gruesome earthly sin (Ps. 40:2–3)—will celebrate the fact that it is all of God's doing in Christ that he now has a song to sing of his complete deliverance (Gal. 1:3–4; Col. 1:13; 1 Thess. 1:10).

Indeed, he will never want to stop singing of the immeasurable riches of the grace and kindness that God has shown to him in Christ (Eph. 2:7–10). And if she is in fact also numbered among God's children, our grief-stricken widow will someday find that God has wiped away her every tear because her Savior has borne all of her griefs and sorrows (Isaiah 53)—and, as inconceivable as it is to her right now, she will join her husband in harmonious songs of thankfulness.[58]

---

[56]See Psalm 13:6: "I will sing to the LORD, because he has dealt bountifully *with me.*"

[57]In a case such as the one that we are considering, there is little doubt that this husband's and father's unwillingness to allow some other Christians to bear the shame of his temptation with him was at least misguided and probably sinful; and there is no doubt that his taking his own life was a very great sin.

[58]I am not claiming that our widow must feel such thankfulness now, when she has not yet gotten sight of the goods that God her Father has prepared for her everlasting enjoyment. We who stand beside those who are currently suffering profoundly should hope and pray that they will, at some point in their earthly lives, begin to glimpse what these goods are and will be, but we are not brutally to demand of them a thankfulness that they cannot yet feel. We must wait patiently with them for God to work this good in them.

The Melody of His Mercy

And so, as it was with the great apostle, as it was with Luther and Calvin, and as it will be with all of God's children, each of us shall someday know that each of the sins that now prick us and all of the sorrows that now stake us down are indeed integral parts of God's glorious plan by which he is tempering everything for our best. For all of this sin and suffering stakes us to the wonders of what God has done for us in Christ.

In a glorious and mysterious way that is currently past our finding out and that in no way excuses our sin, all of this sin and suffering will make it undeniably clear that God's grace—and God's grace alone—is sufficient for us, and thus we shall indeed see that his power is made perfect in our weakness. And therefore it will be our joy and glory in the *eschaton* to sing gladly of our former sin and suffering, so that Christ's power and glory may be more apparent. For God the Father has ordained that the melody of each of our everlasting songs will be how his Son, our glorious Lord, has saved us from all sin and suffering. There the world's broken stage will have been completely renovated, and all of our own badness and brokenness utterly removed.

3

THE SACRED SCRIPT IN THE THEATER OF GOD:

Calvin, the Bible, & the Western World

Douglas Wilson

I begin with a sentiment that I know the other contributors to this volume share, and which I hope the readers share as well. Our business here is to glorify God, not John Calvin. To glorify Calvin at the expense of God's glory would be about the best way I could think of to insult John Calvin, as anyone who knows the central passion of his writings can attest. And why would you want to insult someone in celebration of his five hundredth birthday? In order to honor Calvin rightly, we can hardly neglect one of his foundational emphases.

And to flip this question around the other way, we cannot act as though our concern were to honor Scripture alone and go on to ignore a towering figure like Calvin. What does the Bible say? It says that we are "to respect those who labor among you and are over you in the Lord and admonish you, and to esteem them very highly in love because of their work" (1 Thess. 5:12–13). We can't honor Scripture by refusing to do what it says. So there is no "I am of Paul, I am of Apollos" spirit here—none of that. But there is great thankfulness to God, who gives capable teachers to his church.

The topic before me—John Calvin's relationship to Scripture, and what that relationship did for the Western world—is, given his life calling, an enormous topic. He gave his life to the exposition of Scripture, and because he was both industrious *and* brilliant, there is a mountain of material to consider. So what I want to do is begin with John Calvin's understanding of Scripture, move on to his related view of preaching, and

then show how his view of the supremacy of Scripture affects the task
of preaching in a way that we have lost. It was that view of preaching,
grounded on that view of Scripture, that has placed Western culture so
deeply in debt to the great teacher of Geneva.

CALVIN'S VERY HIGH VIEW OF SCRIPTURE

Let's begin with some things that we might have guessed. Calvin had a
very high view of Scripture. As he said in the *Institutes*,

> Let this be a firm principle: No other word is to be held as the Word of
> God, and given place as such in the church, than what is contained first
> in the Law and the Prophets, then in the writings of the apostles; and the
> only authorized way of teaching in the church is by the prescription and
> standard of his Word.[1]

We have, therefore, an assigned agenda. Comparing the apostles to
their purported successors in the Roman communion, Calvin described
the apostles as being "sure and genuine scribes of the Holy Spirit."[2] In
the course of his discussion of predestination, Calvin said that "Scripture
is the school of the Holy Spirit."[3]

What is obvious to us has been obvious to many other observers as
well. David Steinmetz says, "While Calvin is only too eager to recommend the boundless power of God as a comfort for believers, he does not
want the godly to contemplate that power except through the spectacles
of Scripture. To investigate the will of God apart from the revealed will of
God in the Bible is to lose oneself in a labyrinth of vain speculation."[4]
Who could dare say that Calvin had low views of God's greatness and
sovereignty? At the same time, for Calvin it was never naked philosophical sovereignty. Our only comfort in life and in death is not a syllogism.
God *reveals* himself in creation, in the Scriptures, and ultimately in the
incarnation.

We come to understand his power and majesty by starting with what
he gives, by starting where he invites us to start. We do not start with
an *a priori* God, an infinite Definition in the Sky. We start with a God
who stoops to reveal himself or, as Calvin himself once put it, a God

[1] *Institutes*, 4.8.8.
[2] *Institutes*, 4.8.9.
[3] *Institutes*, 3.21.3.
[4] David Steinmetz, *Calvin in Context* (Oxford: Oxford University Press, 1995), 48.

who lisps. When we spurn this revelation through our sinfulness, it does not alter the fact that God has in fact revealed himself. Blind men do not negate the sun, and deaf men are not usually considered a refutation of the existence of Mozart.

This applies to special revelation, to natural revelation, and to incarnational revelation. Not everyone who looks at the stars believes, not everyone who reads Romans believes, and not everyone in Israel who saw Jesus in the course of his earthly ministry believed. Those forms of revelation, rightly received, are all consistent with one another. They are all given to us by the one triune God with the intent that we receive in faith what he reveals to us. He reveals, and we believe. "For from him and through him and to him are all things" (Rom. 11:36). And because we are bound in sin, we cannot believe unless that also is part of his gift, part of what he reveals. And when we believe rightly, we do not receive what God has done in fragmented pieces. All gifts are tied to the Giver.

Calvin did not divide God's revelation of himself in creation from his revelation of himself in his Word. A man of the revealed word, given to the exposition of it, he also affirmed the reality of natural revelation. J. Daryl Charles put it this way: "While it is sharply debated among Reformed scholars precisely how important in Calvin's writings the natural law is, *that* he affirmed it wholeheartedly is not in question."[5] In the 1930s, Barth and Brunner collided over whether Calvin left any room whatsoever for natural theology. Barth maintained the negative, going only so far as to say that for Calvin it was a possibility in principle but not in fact.[6] But this Barthian take is a category mistake—our failure to read the revelation says nothing whatever about whether the revelation was written. Failure to check the book out of the library does not mean it was never published.

We tend to compartmentalize things in fragmented ways, and this was something Calvin refused to do. He was an integrated thinker, and in this he represented the history of the church well. The university is a Christian idea—where does the *uni* come from? Christ is the *arche*, the integration point of all things (Col. 1:17–18). But we, in our disobedience, have become fragmented thinkers. The *uni*verse is a Christian concept, as is the university. But knowledge is now fragmented, like Humpty

---

[5] J. Daryl Charles, *Retrieving the Natural Law* (Grand Rapids, MI: Eerdmans, 2008), 118n.
[6] Steinmetz, *Calvin in Context*, 23–24.

Dumpty, and our students now attend multiversities, with nothing to tie the knowledge all together. And because of this, our multiversities have become travaversities.

Another example of this healthy mentality is how Calvin refused to divide God from his Word, and how he did not set them at odds with each other. "We owe to the Scripture the same reverence which we owe to God because it has proceeded from Him alone, and has nothing of man mixed with it."[7] Calvin did not set the words of God over *here*, and the person of God himself over *there*. The speaker and the spoken were treated together, considered as one. Calvin refused to fall into the error that Jesus rebuked in the unbelieving Jews of his day—those who searched the Scriptures daily in order to find eternal life, and who searched the Scriptures in such a way as to miss the Person who was that life (John 5:39).

Calvin articulated these high views of Scripture in such a way as to command the respect of those who normally would not give any respect to your average hot gospeler. Barth maintained that "Calvin forged the doctrine of inspiration."[8] On the substance of this claim, we would, of course, have to reject this idea. But just as Anselm formulated a particular view of the atonement without inventing it, so we might say that Calvin shaped the way his heirs talk about inspiration—but it was still the apostle Paul who said that all Scripture is the exhaled breath of God (2 Tim. 3:16). Anticipating a point that is coming shortly, we should perhaps adjust this to say that Calvin shaped the way his heirs *should* be talking about inspiration.

John T. McNeill recognized Calvin's mastery of the Bible's contents and the effect that it had on his exegesis. McNeill said,

> The saving knowledge of God is conveyed to us by the Holy Scripture. Calvin's great resource was his familiarity with the Bible and mastery of its contents. It was impossible for him to know the origins of the books of the Bible as these are known to scholars today [*sic*]. But his talents, training, and religious feeling for the meaning of Scripture were such that much of his interpretation defies the acids of modern critical research.[9]

---

[7]Steven Lawson, *The Expository Genius of John Calvin* (Orlando, FL: Reformation Trust Publishing, 2007), 27.

[8]Karl Barth, *The Theology of John Calvin* (Grand Rapids, MI: Eerdmans, 1995), 167.

[9]John T. McNeill, *The History and Character of Calvinism* (Oxford: Oxford University Press, 1954), 213.

Whatever it was that defied those acids, we should want to get ourselves some of it. Calvin's devotion to Scripture on the practical level, and his dogged commitment to it on the theological level, led Ronald Wallace to contemplate the unthinkable. "All this might seem to justify our ranking Calvin's view on this subject alongside that which is to-day called 'fundamentalism.'"[10] But Wallace pulls out just in time, and what a close call *that* was. "There are, however, other most important considerations which indicate that Calvin did not hold such a view and must qualify our opinion on this matter."[11] But these other examples, when Wallace produces them, are fully consistent with the most robust view of biblical authority possible.

There is a truncated kind of fundamentalism that lives in a world mysteriously shaped *and governed* by modernity, but is in possession of a perfect book, a book in which they find secret coded messages about another world somewhere else, governed on other principles entirely. But robust fundamentalism, of the sort that Wallace tried to rescue Calvin from, avoids this problem entirely. We are coming to this, but in brief it involves the realization that the fundamentals are not the foundation of "our denomination" so much as they are the foundation of all intergalactic realities. In the meantime, those who want to investigate Calvin's understanding of the fundamentals should read through the *Institutes*, 4.2.1–12.

CALVIN'S EXTRAORDINARILY HIGH VIEW OF PREACHING

Moving to the next consideration, it would be safe to say that Calvin's view of preaching was extraordinarily high. My summary of it would be that what the neo-orthodox say about Scripture—that it is a place where you should be prepared to "encounter" the Word of God—Calvin would say about the preaching of the Word. He did not hold that sermons were inspired by the Spirit in the same way the Bible is—obviously. Anyone who wanted to defend the view that all Christian ministers enjoy verbal inspiration in their sermons would be just asking for trouble—the amount of trouble depending on the preacher. But Calvin did maintain that it was still the *Word* that was preached by ministers of the gospel.

---

[10]Ronald Wallace, *Calvin's Doctrine of Word and Sacrament* (Eugene, OR: Wipf and Stock Publishers, 1982), 111.
[11]Ibid.

For example, Calvin said, "This ought to add no small reverence to the Gospel, since we ought not so much to consider men as speaking to us, *as Christ by His own mouth*; for at the time when He promised to publish God's name to men, He had ceased to be in the world; it was not, however, to no purpose that He claimed this office as His own; for He really performs it by His disciples."[12]

What does Calvin think we should expect when we come to hear the Word? "God calls us to Him as if He had His mouth open and we saw Him there in person."[13] Speaking of human teachers, Calvin said, "For among the many excellent gifts with which God has adorned the human race, it is a singular privilege that he deigns to consecrate to himself the mouths and tongues of men in order that his voice may resound in them."[14]

Yeah, buts crowd into our minds instantly, but Calvin is very careful. He places every essential qualification on this. In the first place, he notes that God as "the author of preaching, joining his Spirit with it, promises benefit from it."[15] At the same time, "in mentioning all these things, Paul did not intend to credit to himself even a particle apart from God."[16] We are *not* talking about plenary, verbal inspiration, but we *are* talking about the Holy Spirit ministering his Word and his gospel to the people of God through the preaching of the Scriptures.

This means we have to turn to the relationship between Calvin's high view of Scripture and his high view of preaching. He did not set preaching in opposition to Scripture, as though the word of the church through her ministers had any business competing with the Word of God. A minister should ascend into the pulpit in order to declare what would have been true had he never been born. He is there to preach what was written in the Word before all ages. He is an ambassador, a herald. He is not up there to preach himself, but rather to be a servant who preaches Jesus Christ, the crucified Lord (2 Cor. 4:5). But if the church is in possession of the Word of God, and genuinely believes it to be such, what should this do to the preaching? John Piper has written us an admonition, admirably saying that *brothers, we are not professionals*.[17] I would only want to add that

---

[12]Commentary on Hebrews 2:11, cited in ibid., 83. Emphasis mine.
[13]Sermons on the Epistle to the Ephesians, cited by Lawson, *Expository Genius*, 28.
[14]*Institutes*, 4.1.5.
[15]*Institutes*, 4.1.6.
[16]*Institutes*, 4.1.6.
[17]John Piper, *Brothers, We Are Not Professionals* (Nashville: Broadman and Holman, 2002).

neither are we improv artists. This is where the *script* found in the title of this chapter comes in. Our script is Scripture, and to the extent that we are faithfully representing the lines that God gave to recite and declare, to *that* extent our authority is that of Scripture.

Now the rub. In the battles over the Bible in the twentieth century, and now in the twenty-first century, conservatives moved away from the word *infallible* in favor of *inerrant*. This happened in part because theological liberals had begun using the word *infallible* to mean something more like . . . oh, I don't know, something more like *fallible*. And that reminds me of something else. How is it that liberals preen themselves for the virtues of frankness and honesty when they do things like this to words like *infallible*, or to words like *frank* and *honest* for that matter? Or even words like *liberal*. And now, in the latest go-rounds, the same kind of thing is happening to the word *inerrant*. Men with solemn faces and a shaky donor base affirm the inerrancy of the Bible, and they also affirm that this is not inconsistent with the subtle truth that the Bible has mistakes in it. The serpent was craftier than all the beasts of the field, having completed some post-doctoral work in Europe.

But being wary of liberalism is not enough, and this is where Calvin provides an example to shame and goad us. Those who consider themselves inerrantists, as I most certainly do, need to guard against another mistake that frequently is made in this area. I am convinced that Calvin avoided this particular mistake, but imitating him will involve more than simply avoiding the mistake on paper. The way he dealt with this is, I believe, directly related to the secret of his spiritual authority. It is one of the central reasons why we are in this volume honoring his contributions half a millennium after he made them. But let us not honor him by building a tomb for the prophet, thereby showing whose sons we really are. Let us not be good little "Calvinists," running the floor buffer of pat catechetical answers over the marble of theological genius. This error that we must avoid is a little more subtle than the first one I mentioned—the one that says "not making mistakes" means "making mistakes." That does have a measure of subtlety after a fashion, it is true, and it requires at least three years of graduate studies before someone is able to fall for it. The error I have in mind really is subtle.

One day the schoolmarm in the one-room schoolhouse of modernity gave a test to all the kids in her class. The schoolmarm's name was Mrs.

Enlightenment, and one kid was named the Bhagavad Gita, another was the Koran, another was the Book of Mormon, and of course, a test was also given to the best student in the class, the Holy Bible. When the tests were graded and returned, it turned out that the Bhagavad Gita scored a 38, the Koran a 52, the Book of Mormon a 17, and our Scriptures scored an impressive 97.

What does this make all of us want to do? It makes us want to get up to the teacher's desk pronto and argue for three more points, that's what. We have fallen for the trap of thinking that inerrancy requires us to be grade nerds—always the best student in the class, but one who cannot *abide* making a mistake and who will argue with the teacher over every last point. But something is more fundamentally wrong with this picture than that unfair grading process.

The problem is that the Bible never enrolled in that class and never agreed to be tested by any Mrs. Enlightenment. The Scriptures do not take these tests; the Scriptures *administer* tests. The Bible is not that which *meets* the standard; the Bible is that which *sets* the standard. So would Calvin have agreed that the Bible is like silver, refined sevenfold (Ps. 12:6)? Yes, certainly. Would he have agreed with a score of 97? Of course not. The Scriptures are not a possession of ours, which we may put into the world's balances to be weighed. Rather, the Scriptures are God's scales, in which he places the entire world. They are the scales in which he places heaven and earth, and all the nations. He says to *us*, "*Mene, Mene, Tekel,* and *Parsin*." We do not get to say that to him. The ghostly hand of higher criticism does not get to write anything on the walls of heaven's banqueting halls. And even if it managed that feat, nobody in those halls would be frightened—not even a little bit. There are no heavenly Belshazzars, no celestial knees to knock together.

So what would Calvin have thought of the grade nerds, those who wanted the Scriptures to be perfect in the eyes of the world? Fortunately, we do not have to speculate. He tells us.

> Yet they who strive to build up firm faith in Scripture through disputation are doing things backwards. . . . And if it were a useful labor to refute their cavils, I would with no great trouble shatter the boasts they mutter in their lurking places. But even if anyone clears God's Sacred Word from man's evil speaking, he will not at once imprint upon their hearts that certainty which piety requires. Since for unbelieving men

religion seems to stand by opinion alone, they, in order not to believe anything foolishly or lightly, both wish and demand rational proof that Moses and prophets spoke divinely. But I reply: the testimony of the Spirit is more excellent than all reason.[18]

A man argued into the kingdom can be argued out of it. If, however, he is converted to God, nothing can separate him from the love of God in Christ Jesus. Calvin's view of reason here is no more against reason than not letting kindergartners take calculus is against calculus. There are *prerequisites*. Calvin also says,

> Let this point therefore stand: that those whom the Holy Spirit has inwardly taught truly rest upon Scripture, and that Scripture indeed is self-authenticated: hence, it is not right to subject it to proof and reasoning.[19]

And a bit later:

> Unless this certainty, higher and stronger than any human judgment, be present, it will be vain to fortify the authority of Scripture by arguments, to establish it by common agreement of the church, or to confirm it with other helps.[20]

But please mark this well. Calvin is *not* embracing a blind-leap fideism. He is not telling us to take this view of Scripture simply because we want to, or need to. He says above that if refuting these cavils would be useful, he would have no trouble doing so. He would have no trouble showing that the three points were rightfully ours. But he would also have no trouble showing Mrs. Enlightenment that unbelief ought not to be teaching that class or grading the papers. He is not after those three points. He is after Mrs. Enlightenment's *job*.

So Calvin has no problem with reasonable arguments. He has no problem respecting them in their proper place. This is how he put it:

> Conversely, once we have embraced [Scripture] devoutly as its dignity deserves, and have recognized it to be above the common sort of things, those arguments—not strong enough before to engraft and fix the certainty of Scripture in our minds—become very useful aids.[21]

---

[18]*Institutes*, 1.7.4.
[19]*Institutes*, 1.7.4.
[20]*Institutes*, 1.8.1.
[21]*Institutes*, 1.8.1.

This is no mere detail. It is the difference between having a geocentric view of the solar system and a heliocentric view. John Calvin wrote, taught, and preached as though the Bible were the sun around which everything else revolved. The law of the Lord is perfect, and it runs its course in the same way that the sun does (Ps. 19:4–7). With an open Bible in his hands, he was therefore able to assume the center. Those who understand him do the same. As a preacher, he could assume the center because he held in his hands that which *was* the center. We have drifted far away from this, and we have done all that drifting with what we know to be a perfect book in our hands. How could this happen?

Our debates over the inerrancy of the Bible tend to be limited to the question of how *pure* the sun is. We take on those who say the sunspots are blemishes, and we argue the point with them, sometimes very effectively. We have books with titles like *The Sunspot Fallacies*. We have worldview seminars in the summer to teach our young people that sunspots are not faults or failings at all. And there is no question that, as far as *that* issue goes, John Calvin would be with us on the perfection of the sun.

But there is another issue—one that we have almost entirely neglected in our day. What good is a perfect sun if it revolves around a very imperfect earth and all its tawdry corruptions? What good to us is a perfect sun orbiting us at greater and greater distances out, so that now in the twenty-first century it almost appears as a star? John Calvin believed the sun was perfect, certainly, but *his* solar system was *logocentric*—everything else revolved around the word (*logos*), everything was seen in the light that it gave, everything was warmed by the heat that came from it.

The doctrine of *sola Scriptura* has two components, and of late we evangelicals have been contending for only one of them. The Bible, and only the Bible, as Keith Mathison has demonstrated, is the *ultimate* and *infallible* spiritual authority in the lives of believers.[22] We have fought a series of skirmishes over the latter. Conservative evangelicals believe the Bible has no mistakes in it, whether you call that freedom from error *infallibility* or *inerrancy*. And rightly so. But who today believes and speaks as Calvin did? Who treats the Bible as Calvin did? Who today thinks that the Bible open in the pulpit is a lit stick of divine dynamite, one that mere mortals are ordained and authorized to throw out into the

---

[22]Keith Mathison, *The Shape of Sola Scriptura* (Moscow, ID; Canon Press, 2001).

world? How many preachers have sermons on file that they would not dare to preach without purchasing some extra life insurance first?

Our view of Scripture needs to take practical account of both of these issues—what is the *purity* of the sun, certainly, but also what is the *place* of the sun? If we want to learn Reformation basics from John Calvin, this is what we need to recover. An important issue concerns the nature of God's Word, but in our day the thing we are really clueless about is the authoritative *centrality* of God's Word.

To complicate matters, some modern Christians want to divide it up and be heliocentric on matters of personal piety and confessionalism, while being geocentric with regard to any matters involving the public square. I confess that I am not up to this challenge because my math is not that good. Talk about your epicycles.

Our battles over infallibility and/or inerrancy are recent, fresh, and ongoing. Keep fighting *that* fight, and well done. As we used to say back in the day, keep on keeping on. But we wandered away from heliocentrism centuries ago, and may God have mercy on his languishing church. If we come to recover this by grace through faith, the impact on preachers of the Word would be enormous. Let Calvin describe what that should be like. This is from Book 4 of the *Institutes*:

> Here, then, is the sovereign power with which the pastors of the church, by whatever name they be called, ought to be endowed. That is that they may dare boldly to do all things by God's Word; may compel all worldly power, glory, wisdom, and exaltation to yield to and obey his majesty; supported by his power, may command all from the highest even to the last; may build up Christ's household and cast down Satan's; may feed the sheep and drive away the wolves; may instruct and exhort the teachable; may accuse, rebuke, and subdue the rebellious and stubborn; may bind and loose; finally, if need be, may launch thunderbolts and lightnings, but do all things in God's Word.[23]

This is the endowment of pastors. *All* things in God's Word. If that sounds grand and inspiring, that is good because that is exactly what it is. But if it also sounds terrifying and is coming across like a surefire career wrecker, then you are probably closer to grasping what it actually means. Cornelius Van Til showed himself Calvin's true heir when he said that

---

[23] *Institutes*, 4.8.9.

this book is authoritative in everything it addresses . . . and it addresses everything.

SCRIPTURE, PREACHING, AND THE WORLD

So to conclude, what do we have? What have we learned? John Calvin understood what the Scriptures were like, and he knew what the Scriptures were given to us to do. The entire world is a theater in which the majesty of God is displayed. General revelation is that theater, and a glorious theater it is. Special revelation is God's holy script. We are not supposed to be extemporaneous actors trying to figure out our lines by looking at the embellishments and scrollwork near the ceiling of the theater. We have a script in our hands, and in this script we are given our lines.

In addition, Christ in his grace has given gifts to men, and among those gifts is the fact that he has made some men directors. This theater was built for this play, and this play was written to be performed in this theater. The job of the director is to keep people from wandering off the point. We need to stay on task. Other actors and directors from other stage companies loudly maintain that the theater is really theirs, that their scripts are better, their plotlines starker and grittier, their shows make more money, and in all this their rebellion is complete.

In sum, our view of Scripture drives our view of preaching, and our preaching drives the world. If the world is not in fact driven, then we need to work our way back up the drivetrain and ask ourselves some hard questions.

What are we to do? We are to recognize where we are, where God has placed us, and we are to speak our lines *in faith*. We are not to murmur; we must speak them out. If we are to speak in faith, what is that faith? What does this faith do? What is it that *overcomes the world?* Is it not our faith (1 John 5:4)? We lament, *Why does the world not believe?* Well, when was the last time we *commanded* it to? When was the last time we spoke with authority, and not like the scribes?

Faith comes by hearing and hearing by the word of Christ (Rom. 10:17). How will they believe without a preacher, and how will they preach unless they are sent? Sent to do what? We were not sent to preach about the perfections of a perfect but distant star, cool and twinkling against a black, velvet sky. We were not even sent to preach a moon, reflecting derivative light—we are not servants of the ruler of the evening. We were sent to preach a blazing sun, one that lights and heats every creature, one that dominates all things, and one around which *everything* must of necessity revolve.

A REAL MINISTRY

We were not sent to clear our throats nervously, trying to get somebody's attention. We were not sent in order to make a few mild suggestions. We were not sent to indulge in a few postmodern dabblings of a theological nature. We were commissioned—I believe the word is *ordained*—to compel every manifestation of worldly power, glory, wisdom, and exaltation to yield to and obey the majesty of God, in full accordance with God's Word. We were ordained to feed the sheep and drive away wolves, and all by God's Word. We were sent to bind and loose, and all by God's Word. And if need be, we have been ordained to open the Word completely, press it flat against the pulpit, hold on to both sides of that pulpit, pray for divine protection, and preach as though we were thunder and lightning. How could we not? The Scriptures are a great thunderhead.

Is this bombast? Is this self-flattery? For some it is like fighting some historical battle over again, along with other costumed reenactors. For some it is just playing Reformation dressup. But may God have mercy on us and give us what only he can give. He did exactly this for John Calvin and, five hundred years later, we are still talking about it.

And so I give you John Calvin, servant of God in Geneva, a real man made out of real clay. But he had a real heart, and he held a real Bible in his hands. And because of that, being a servant of a real God, he had what we should call a real ministry.

4

THE SECULAR SCRIPT IN THE THEATER OF GOD:

Calvin on the Christian Meaning of Public Life

Marvin Olasky

It is a privilege to contribute this chapter in honor of a man, John Calvin, who wrote an enormously influential book. He did not go by what everyone was saying. He read what God's authors had written in the Bible. He instructed his flock to ignore much of the received theological and political wisdom of the time. In this chapter, I would like to concentrate on some things Calvin taught about the Christian meaning of public life that *contradicted* what just about everyone else at the time was saying.

FINDING MESSIAH

Let me begin with something from my own life. As some of you know, I did not have the advantage of growing up in a Christian home and knowing from an early age the basics of what is true. I grew up in a Judaism that emphasized following old customs, not thinking about what was true. During the 1960s, I gravitated to whatever I heard that seemed cool. I became an atheist. I participated in antiwar demonstrations. I cared about the poor in an abstract way.

Then I went further, joining the Communist Party in 1972. I studied Russian to speak with my Soviet big brothers. In 1974, though, I picked up a copy of the New Testament in Russian and started reading it just to improve my humble Russian language skills—or so I thought. I read very slowly, so it took me a while to get to chapter 4 of Matthew.

That is where I read something striking: Satan tempts Jesus three times. Each time Jesus responds, "It is written." This interested me as a writer: Jesus cared enough about a book to emphasize its writing—even when offered magnificent prizes if he would act according to what he had just heard.

"IT IS WRITTEN"

Up to that time I briefly had encountered two variants of what passed as Christian practice. Growing up in Boston, I had heard Roman Catholics purportedly taking care of their sin by repeating Hail Marys. At college in New Haven, I had heard William Sloane Coffin criticizing the war in Vietnam, so I associated liberal Protestantism with antiwar demonstrations. But here Jesus was saying something radically different. *It is written.*

Eventually, purely through God's grace—I was not seeking but completely lost—I gained some faith in Jesus and in 1976 joined a church. That was the year of an evangelistic campaign in which people wore buttons saying, "I Found It." That's what I heard—people saying, *I* found it.

But in 1977, a Reformed pastor in essence told me that what I had heard was theologically incorrect. I knew from my personal experience that I had not found it, since God in his mercy had drawn me to himself. The little theology I knew (only later did I learn that there was a difference between Arminian and Armenian) contradicted my experience and, more importantly, what is written in the Bible. The pastor took me through Romans over several days of tutoring. Then I read Calvin's *Institutes of the Christian Religion* and saw that he emphasized not what the pontiff said but what is written, in God's special book.

My point is this: We should not go by what we hear. We should go by what is written, and particularly by what Christ and his apostles taught. This is remarkable. Five centuries ago just about everyone went by what they heard. Ordinary people in Europe, with the exception of Jews—and there is little about Jewish history that is ordinary—were illiterate. The Roman Catholic Church viewed this not as a minus but a plus: The view was that if people read the Bible, they would become confused, so they should merely listen to their priests and do what the priests said.

HOW CALVIN CHALLENGED CONVENTIONAL WISDOM

John Piper recently has written about William Tyndale's contribution and Thomas More's attacks on Tyndale.[1] John writes, "Thomas More's criticism of Tyndale boils down mainly to the way Tyndale translated five words. He translated *presbuteros* as elder instead of priest. He translated *ekklesia* as congregation instead of church. He translated *metanoeo* as repent instead of do penance. He translated *exomologeo* as acknowledge or admit instead of confess. And he translated *agape* as love instead of charity."[2] John Calvin did something similar in his *Institutes* and other writings, not by translating but by exegeting. He brought back the Christian meaning of public life, after the medieval church had essentially stripped it of meaning and said that only ecclesiastical life was significant. He particularly changed thinking about the role of Christians in government and in entrepreneurial activity. Tyndale translated five words. So we will look at five ways in each of these two areas, government and business/economics, where Calvin challenged the conventional wisdom.

CHRISTIANS AND GOVERNMENT

1) Sacred Politics

First, many Christians throughout medieval times had heard that work in a church or life in a monastery was the best way to follow God's will. The theater of God, in short, was not the whole world but only the parts of it where priests removed themselves from the world. But Calvin wrote in his *Institutes*, book 4, chapter 20—other quotations in this section also come from there unless otherwise noted—"No one ought to doubt that civil authority is a calling not only holy and lawful before God, but also the most sacred and by far the most honorable of all callings in the whole life of mortal men." Such thinking led many of the founders of the American republic to enter politics.

2) The Cleanness of the Courts

Second, many Christians throughout medieval times had heard that they should not go to court. One result was that the weak had little redress against the powerful. Submission to church and state authority was a

---

[1]John Piper, *Filling Up the Afflictions of Christ: The Cost of Bringing the Gospel to the Nations in the Lives of William Tyndale, Adoniram Judson, and John Paton* (Wheaton, IL: Crossway, 2009), 27–52.
[2]Ibid., 49.

Christian duty. Any back talk in court or otherwise was rebellion against God. But Calvin wrote, "As for those who strictly condemn all legal contentions, let them realize that they therewith repudiate God's holy ordinance, and one of the class of gifts that can be clean to the clean. . . . The Christian endures insults, but with amity and equity defends the public interest. . . . [He will use] the help of the magistrate in preserving their own possessions." Such thinking led Americans to push for a government of laws, not of men.

3) Kings under Authority

Third, many Christians throughout medieval times had heard that rulers and magistrates could do virtually whatever they want. The powerful were bound only by their own power, and their edicts were not to be challenged by Scripture. Calvin, though, wrote that "kings should not multiply horses for themselves; nor set their mind upon avarice. . . . [Princes] should remember that their revenues are not so much their private chests as the treasuries of the entire people which cannot be squandered or despoiled without manifest injustice." He argued, "If [note the *if*] kings want to be considered legitimate and as servants of God, they need to show that they are real fathers to their nation." Such thinking led Americans in the 1760s and 1770s to argue that taxation without representation was tyranny, because they had a right to decide how their taxes should be levied and spent.

4) Choosing One's Leaders

Fourth, Christians throughout medieval times had almost never been able to vote for leaders, but in exegeting Deuteronomy 1:14–16 Calvin stated that

> those who were to preside in judgment were not appointed only by the will of Moses, but elected by the votes of the people. And this is the most desirable kind of liberty, that we should not be compelled to obey every person who may be tyrannically put over our heads; but which allows of election, so that no one should rule except he be approved by us. And this is further confirmed in the next verse, wherein Moses recounts that he awaited the consent of the people, and that nothing was attempted which did not please them all.

Calvin also argued, in his commentary on Micah, that it is "the best condition of the people, when they can choose, by common consent, their own shepherds. . . . [W]hen men become kings by hereditary right, it seems not consistent with liberty." In commenting on Acts, Calvin wrote, "It is tyrannous if any one man appoint or make ministers at his pleasure." Such thinking led the American founders to establish a republic. They knew that, given sin, few kings could resist robbing and even killing to get what they wanted.

5) The Right to Rebel

Before they could establish freedom to choose, though, the founders had a problem: *What loyalty did they owe to the king?* That question leads to my fifth and final point in this section. Many Christians throughout medieval times had heard that it would be unbiblical to rebel against those said to rule by divine right, but Calvin, while arguing against private individuals taking the law into their own hands, wrote about "magistrates of the people, appointed to restrain the willfulness of kings." He wrote that such magistrates must not "wink at kings who violently fall upon and assault the lowly common folk." He wrote that a refusal to oppose monarchs in such situations is "nefarious perfidy, because they dishonestly betray the freedom of the people, of which they know that they have been appointed protectors by God's ordinance."

Calvin in his writing did not stretch out that doctrine. His most notable defense of rebellion concerned one of the greatest aggressions in history: Pharaoh's order that all Hebrew babies be killed. Calvin in his commentary on Exodus defended the Hebrew midwives who disobeyed. He wrote that obedience in this situation was "preposterously unwise." He argued that those who obeyed were attempting to "gratify the transitory kings of earth" while taking "no account of God." Calvin largely defended rebellion to preserve life.

His disciples, facing a murderous monarch, went further. Roman Catholic aggression had its major sixteenth-century manifestation in the so-called St. Bartholomew's Day Massacre, which began on August 23, 1572, and ended with the murder by governmental decree of anywhere from five thousand to sixty thousand Huguenots (estimates vary widely). That tragedy precipitated new declarations of the right to oppose kings. One Calvin disciple in 1579 wrote *Vindiciae contra Tyran-os* ("Vindication against

Tyrants"), which contended that even military revolt might be necessary to defend God's law against kings who give orders contrary to it.

This was a huge change. The author of *Vindiciae* argued that fundamental law comes from God, so obeying the law means obeying God, not necessarily the state. Rebellion against an unlawful state act, led by "lesser magistrates" such as local leaders, was thus a justifiable maintenance of true law. Those in power did not readily relinquish medieval thinking. In England, for example, even a diminishing of royal authority did not quickly bring about freedom: English lawyers joked that "parliament can do everything except making a woman a man, or a man a woman." But as generation after generation of Calvinists read *Vindiciae* or other works that emphasized the limitations of power, the idea of government-almost-like-God diminished.

I will not trace here the influence from the sixteenth through eighteenth centuries, because David W. Hall does a good job of that in his book *Calvin in the Public Square*. Many contributed through the decades: Pienne Viret, John Ponet, Christopher Goodman, John Knox, Theodore Beza, Hubert Languet and Philippe du Plessis Mornay, Lambert Daneau, Johannes Althusius, Samuel Rutherford—and the list continues to Samuel Adams, who in 1743 defended his Harvard thesis that resistance to the supreme magistrate was lawful "if the Commonwealth cannot otherwise be preserved." According to John Adams and many others, Calvin's doctrines greatly influenced Americans of the 1760s and 1770s.

So, to sum up some of Calvin's thoughts in this area: Sin is always with us, but work in politics and law can at times glorify God. Monarchies can and probably will be ungodly. Republics are better. Since both rulers and ruled are sinners, limited government is the best help to both. When leaders try to be dictators, lesser magistrates—when a tipping point arises—can be righteously rebellious.

CHRISTIANS AS ENTREPRENEURS

Now we turn to the difference between what Christians had previously heard about work and economics and what Calvin wrote.

1) Honest Labor Glorifies God

First and most obvious, Calvin emphasized that all honest labor, not just that within churches and monasteries, glorifies God. We take this for granted now, but for centuries those engaged in ordinary life had heard that they were leading a second-class existence.

Calvin emphasized taking dominion over all creation, not just ecclesiastical acreage. In a sermon on Matthew 3, Calvin envisioned God as "beckoning with his finger and saying to each and every individual, 'I want you to live this way or that.'" *Each and every* person, not just the priest, has a God-given vocation that was "good and profitable for the common good." Work itself is not a curse, and no work done unto God is secular.

2) No Need for Added Discipline

Second, Christians throughout medieval times had heard that the way to get closer to God was through some added-on disciplines such as penance, fasting, and other forms of self-flagellation. But Calvin wrote that God did not require such celebrations of discipline, especially when it took productive discipline for Christians to earn their daily bread and to help others. Calvin knew that requiring what could be called "hard practice" beyond the hardness of life itself could lead to harmful pride and to a wasting of talents.

I said "what could be called" not because Calvin used the words "hard practice," but because I spent some time a few years back with Japanese Buddhists who immersed themselves in freezing mountain streams or sat for hours in the lotus position without moving, until their legs cramped up and they could hardly walk. I remember one woman in her forties who had lived a hard life with abandonment by her parents and then her husband. She had one child. When he was a toddler, she began coming to a Shingon Buddhist temple on Mount Koya-san and engaging in hard practice—but it struck me that taking care of a two-year-old was hard practice in itself. Calvin in essence asked the question, *Why substitute unproductive and unnecessary hard practice for productive hard practice?*

Calvin showed that the real way to get closer to God is to do what God has made us to do. If I say, "I want to go to Chicago this evening, and this is a bad laptop because it does not have an engine and seats that will get me there," I am obviously misunderstanding the purpose of a laptop. Calvin linked anthropology and teleology. He wrote in his commentary on Genesis 2,

> Men were created to employ themselves in some work, and not to lie down in inactivity and idleness. When God ordained that men should be exercised in the culture of the ground, he condemned, in his own person, all indolent response. . . . Nothing is more contrary to the order of nature than to consume life in eating, drinking, and sleeping.

God makes us to work. Commenting on Deuteronomy 24, Calvin argued that a removal of work "would throw human life into ruin." Today many people who retire while still in good health find that out. Calvin, with many kinds of health problems, wrote and preached until he died. He proposed, and modeled in his life, the discipline of work in a calling, and the discipline of service, particularly to the poor. His hard practice emphasized the discipline of getting up early and working through the day, with frequent preaching and an astounding output of writing in those days when the cutting edge of word processing was a quill pen.

3) Improving the Christian Understanding of Business

Third, Calvin's stress on the importance of work led him to promote vastly improved Christian understanding of what can and should be achieved through business. My sense is that we can see five levels of understanding:

Level 1 is what some Christians then and now have grudgingly believed: Work gets us our daily bread but has little value beyond that.

Level 2 also grudgingly supports work because cash thus acquired can go to support ministries and missions.

Level 3 support of work is semigrudging because a job supports a family and ministries and also allows workers to witness to coworkers.

Calvin does not neglect those pragmatic uses of work and adds one more, which we could call Level 4—stewardship that improves what we are given and creates multigenerational wealth. In discussing Genesis, Calvin advises his readers, "Let him who possesses a field so partake of its yearly fruits that he may not suffer the ground to be injured by his negligence, but let him endeavor to hand it down to posterity as he received it, or even better cultivated."

We should add to that a Level 5: Building a business is more than a means to an end. Americans employed outside the home typically spend more of their active time at their places of work than anywhere else.

Those places can be where individuals gain dignity, grasp freedom, and employ creativity, or they can be domains of forced labor without joy. If the latter, they breed elder brothers—playing off the parable of the prodigal son—who resent what only seems like obligation. (And younger brothers who see their elders in what seems like slavish conformity will often run away. That's one reason why, in the United States, 1950s culture mutated into 1960s culture. But I digress.)

4) The Proper Use of Credit

Let's return to Calvin and a fourth point related to economics: He understood that building businesses and work opportunities required the proper use of credit, and that the medieval church's interpretation of usury was wrong. Christians throughout medieval times had heard that they should not make loans involving the charging of interest—and as a result Christians made few business loans. (Jews made loans and became the objects of envy and popular rage.)

Calvin, though, argued that biblical opposition to usury was not to all interest-bearing loans but to those that took advantage of the poor. He understood that loans to grow a business were different than loans to a starving man—and that charging interest on the former was legitimate. He understood that banning interest in regular economic activity reduced opportunities to promote business expansion and human flourishing. Calvin's defense of interest was important in his day and may seem to be unchallenged now, but Muslim emphasis on sharia law, which purportedly bans interest, makes his arguments topical again.

5) Love, Not Charity

Fifth, many people throughout medieval times had heard that the best way to help the poor was to give them spare food, clothes, and coins. Tyndale's emphasis on *agape* rather than charity challenged that, and Calvin's theoretical writing, plus the policies he implemented in Geneva, showed in practice the meaning of *agape*. He taught and showed that the best way to tackle poverty was not to distribute alms but to open a business and employ those who would otherwise beg.

The understanding underlying Calvin's emphasis on helping the poor and the alien was simple: Everyone is created in God's image and is worthy of respect. He wrote,

> We cannot but behold our own face as it were in a glass in the person that is poor and despised . . . though he were the furthest stranger in the world. Let a Moor or a Barbarian come among us, and yet inasmuch as he is a man, he brings with him a looking glass wherein we may see that he is our brother and neighbor.

The formula was not hard: God creates, man respects.

Over time, however, some Christians stopped fighting poverty and even began to see it as a road to holiness. They leaped from the biblical argument that the love of money is a root of all kinds of evil to a belief that money and material things in themselves are evil. They took vows of poverty and went begging from city to city, thinking this would draw them and the almsgivers closer to God. Shortly before Calvin's birth, a French bishop invited beggars from all over Europe to come to his city of Lyon so church members could more readily win salvation by contribution. Soon local resources were overtaxed, and people were dying in the streets. Church leaders had to call the whole thing off.

NEITHER POVERTY NOR RICHES

Calvin favored neither hair shirts nor indulgent charity. He showed that voluntary poverty arose within a wrongheaded salvation-by-works mentality. The Catholic Church in medieval times sometimes romanticized poverty. The same condescending error occurs today, but Calvin in his commentary on the book of Amos noted that poverty does not make people godly—and might even make them more susceptible to Satan's snares: "When men are pressed by famine, they would sooner sell their lives a hundred times that they may save themselves from hunger, no matter what the price." Instead of emphasizing the transfer of food, Calvin encouraged new businesses, particularly weaving. He taught that all vocations except those forbidden by God (such as assassin-for-hire) are good.

Geneva's war on poverty mirrored Calvin's emphasis on productive hard practice. To make sure that real needs (and only real needs) were met, the city of twelve thousand had twenty-eight districts, each with a population of about 425. A district supervisor screened all requests and presented to the deacons any he thought deserved approval. Deacons visited homes to verify needs. About 5 percent of Geneva's population received financial help, almost always short-term. Deacons, thinking entrepreneurially, sometimes used church funds to pay for tools, raw materials, and the initial rent on a shop. Refugees who were craftsmen could get to work.

To sum up this section, all honest labor (not just church work) is good. Self-flagellation is bad. We don't need to make life harder than it is. Hard work is good, and interest-bearing loans that help businesses to expand and provide more work are good. The poor should work rather than beg, receiving start-up help as needed. No help should be given to the able but lazy. This was Calvin's model, and social Calvinism became the American way, until social Darwinism and social universalism arose in the late nineteenth century.

PAYING ATTENTION TO THE WORLD

We've looked at both politics and economics as stages in the theater of God, but I would like to emphasize the fundamental way in which Calvin undercut what Christians had heard from centuries of priests: He told his followers that they were in the theater of God. He instructed his followers to pay attention to the events around them. That may not seem like much, but artists and writers patronized by the medieval Catholic Church deliberately did not pay attention. "Look at the birds of the air," Jesus told his disciples, but artists either did not look or did not help others to look.

The reason for not looking: Realism was virtually a heresy. It was no accident nor lack of knowledge of how to use perspective in drawing that led to generic figures floating off the earth in medieval artwork. The overall goal was to separate from this world. So artists depicted separated saints. But Calvin's emphasis on providence meant that daily events give us some indication of God's mind at work and play. "If God does nothing random, there must always be something to learn," Calvin wrote. Wanting to learn, and considering the world important, Calvinists founded newspapers, colleges, and scientific societies.

Calvinistic mindfulness included paying attention to surrounding languages. Christian intellectuals had heard for centuries that they should write in Latin, but Calvin wrote in French as well and preached in a way accessible to the broad public, not just scholars. His sentences were short and clear, a change from lugubrious prose so remarkable that historians of language see Calvin as the creator of modern French sentence structure.

Christians throughout medieval times had heard that they were holier if they abstained from all material pleasures. Calvin, though, wrote that God "meant not only to provide for necessity but also for delight and good cheer. . . . Has the Lord clothed the flowers with the great beauty that greets our eyes, the sweetness of smell that is wafted upon our nostrils, and yet will it be unlawful for our eyes to be affected by that beauty, or our sense of smell by the sweetness of that odor?" He opposed any doctrine that "deprives us of the lawful fruit of God's beneficence."

Calvin was a fallen sinner as all of us are. He clearly had his weaknesses—but those weaknesses often grew out of strengths. Amoral libertines have attacked him for centuries, but so have limited-government libertarians, who criticize regulations that the Geneva city council, sometimes at odds with Calvin but nevertheless under his tutelage, passed during the last decade of Calvin's life. For example, starting in 1558, dinners of all kinds were to include no more than three courses, each course having a maximum of four different dishes. Starting in 1560, the wearing of gold or silver necklaces, along with other jewelry, was also forbidden.

Calvin supported such restrictions and may have proposed some. His reasons were public-spirited: He wanted native Genevans to spend less money on themselves and provide more help to the poor refugees who flooded into Switzerland, as France persecuted Protestants who eventually outnumbered the native Genevans. Calvin reacted as many American Christians would if the United States now had over three hundred million immigrants living in great poverty, while the owners of Park Avenue penthouses regularly put on parties for pooches.

Furthermore, Calvin had seen the affluent sometimes strip the indebted poor of their furniture and even their clothes. He could not stomach grand parties and rich clothes—"Jesus Christ was not a tailor," he said—when others were starving and dressed in rags. He wanted the rich to dress simply and spend the money they saved on new businesses that would employ the poor. But such changes need to come through changed hearts. Attempts to force compassion foster resentment.

Calvin and Calvinists made other errors when they attempted to use state power to force biblical ways of living. Calvin himself knew the limitations of power. He wrote in his commentary on John that "the kingdom of Christ, being spiritual, must be founded on the doctrine and power of the Spirit. In the same manner, too, its edification is promoted; for neither the laws and edicts of men, nor the punishments inflicted by them, enter into the consciences." If Calvin had always kept that in mind, he might have been able to avoid some of his infamous incidents, such as the killing of Michael Servetus that he did not order but did not oppose. That, for some, overpowers the good that he did.

Calvin showed more flexibility in thinking about laws than his reputation suggests. For example, some Christians demand that ancient Israel's civil law must be our own, but Calvin attacked "perilous and seditious" notions that modern states must adopt "the political system of Moses." He wrote that while all should follow God's moral law, "Constitutions have certain circumstances under which they in part depend. It therefore does not matter that they are different, provided all equally press toward the same goal of equity." He wrote that "the statement of some, that the law of God given through Moses is dishonored when it is abrogated and new laws preferred to it, is utterly vain."

Here we see Calvin's fundamental understanding of secular scripts within the theater of God. He knew that a stimulating theater stages a variety of dramas, and many are tragedies. He allowed room for cultural differences that laws would reflect. He wrote, "How malicious and hateful toward public welfare would a man be who is offended by such diversity." He demanded only that the state allow people to worship God and not violate "that conscience which God has engraved upon the minds of men."

Today, surrounded by media cacophony, we hear all kinds of things, and we all have a tendency to repeat what others say. We have leading politicians who go around talking up vain imaginings. This country would be stronger and better if we paused to look at what is written. What is written in the Bible. What is written in a Constitution that is grounded in biblical thinking. What is written in the books of the Bible's finest interpreter, John Calvin. Our national leaders should especially hear Calvin's admonition that they "are ordained protectors and vindicators of public innocence. . . . Their sole endeavor should be to provide for the common safety and peace of all."

5

LIVING WITH
ONE FOOT RAISED:

Calvin on the Glory of the Final
Resurrection & Heaven

Sam Storms

On August 5, 1563, John Calvin wrote a letter of encouragement and counsel to Madame de Coligny, the wife of one of the more important leaders of the Protestant Reformation in France. She had recently recovered from a struggle with numerous physical afflictions. In direct reference to her diseases, and all of ours as well, Calvin said,

> They [that is, our physical afflictions and diseases] should, moreover, serve us for medicines to purge us from worldly affections, and retrench [i.e., remove] what is superfluous in us, and since they are to us the messengers of death, we ought to learn to have *one foot raised* to take our departure when it shall please God.[1]

We ought to learn from our physical afflictions, said Calvin, to live every day with "one foot raised" to take our departure into heaven when it shall please God. Do we live every day with one foot lifted ever so deftly off the ground in constant alert and anxious expectation of the moment when we will depart this world and enter into the splendor of heaven and the presence of God himself? I strongly suspect that Calvin did and that there is much about living in expectation of that day that we can learn from him.

Calvin is a remarkably helpful guide, a man of great wisdom, insight,

---

[1] John Calvin, *Selected Works*, Vol. 7, 1551, ed. H. Beveridge and J. Bonnet (Grand Rapids, MI: Baker, 1983), 331ff. (emphasis mine).

and personal energy when it comes to thinking about the resurrection of the body and our anticipation of eternal life in the new heavens and new earth. We see this in no fewer than four ways.

A PILGRIM ON THIS EARTH

First, Calvin was in the truest sense of the term a *pilgrim* on this earth. Calvin knew from personal experience what it meant to be a *sojourner* and an *exile* in this life.[2] As he reflected on Paul's exhortation in Colossians 3:1 that we "seek the things that are above," he argued that only in doing so shall we embrace our identity as "sojourners in this world," that is to say, people who "are not bound to it."[3]

Nowhere does this emphasis in Calvin come out with greater clarity than in his comments on Hebrews 11 and 13. Calvin concludes from 11:16 (where the author mentions the patriarchs' "desire" for "a better country, that is, a heavenly one") "that there is no place for us among God's children, except we renounce the world, and that there will be for us no inheritance in heaven, except we become pilgrims on earth."[4] His observations on 13:14 are especially instructive. There the author of Hebrews describes the perspective of all believers in saying: "For here [i.e., on this earth] we have no lasting city, but we seek the city that is to come." In light of this, says Calvin, we should consider that

> we have no fixed residence but in heaven. Whenever, therefore, we are driven from place to place, or whenever any change happens to us, let us think of what the Apostle teaches us here, that we have no certain abode on earth, for heaven is our inheritance; and when more and more tried, let us ever prepare ourselves for our last end; for they who enjoy a very quiet life commonly imagine that they have a rest in this world: it is hence profitable for us, who are prone to this kind of sloth, to be often tossed here and there, that we who are too much inclined to look on things below, may learn to turn our eyes up to heaven.[5]

---

[2]In his commentary on 1 Peter 2:11, Calvin describes the children of God, wherever they may be, as "only *guests* in this world" (*Commentaries on the Catholic Epistles,* trans. and ed. the Rev. John Owen [Grand Rapids, MI: Baker Book House, 2005], Vol. 22, 78; emphasis mine). Two of the more recent biographies of Calvin have recognized this about him. Note the subtitles in both W. Robert Godfrey, *John Calvin: Pilgrim and Pastor* (Wheaton: Crossway, 2009) and Herman J. Selderhuis, *John Calvin: A Pilgrim's Life* (Downers Grove: IVP, 2009).

[3]John Calvin, *Commentaries on the Epistles of Paul the Apostle to the Philippians, Colossians, and Thessalonians,* trans. the Rev. John Pringle (Grand Rapids, MI: Baker Book House, 2005), Vol. 21, 205.

[4]John Calvin, *Commentaries on the Epistle of Paul the Apostle to the Hebrews,* trans. the Rev. John Owen (Grand Rapids, MI: Baker Book House, 2005), Vol. 22, 285.

[5]Ibid., 349.

This keen sense of being a pilgrim and sojourner on earth was reinforced in Calvin's heart by the harsh realities of his life. Forced to flee Paris because of his inflammatory remarks about the Roman Catholic Church and the need for reform, Calvin is reported to have descended from a window by means of bedsheets and escaped from the city disguised as a vinedresser with a hoe on his shoulder. The next two years were spent as a wandering student and evangelist. He settled in Basel, hoping to spend his life in quiet study. Calvin returned to Paris in 1536 to settle some old financial matters. He decided to go from there to Strasbourg to be a scholar, but as a result of his famous encounter with William Farel, ended up in Geneva. Trouble erupted when he and Farel sought to administer church discipline and to restrict access to the Lord's Table to those who were spiritually qualified. The two were literally kicked out of town in April 1538.

Calvin was determined to return to Basel and resume his studies, but Martin Bucer (who was won to the Reformation while listening to Luther at the Leipzig debate in 1519) persuaded him to come to Strasbourg. Evidently Bucer was having a difficult time at first persuading Calvin to come to Strasbourg. He sent word to Farel, asking his advice on how to deal with the matter. "Pronounce the wrath of God," said Farel. In a thunderous letter to Calvin, Bucer wrote, "God will know how to find a rebellious servant, even as he found Jonah!" Frightened by the comparison with Jonah, Calvin reluctantly said yes and went to Strasbourg.

There he taught theology and trained candidates for the ministry while working on a revision of his *Institutes* and writing a commentary on Romans. He also pastored the church in the city and was convinced Strasbourg would be his permanent home. But the situation in Geneva had deteriorated. The political forces sympathetic to Calvin had regained power and issued him an urgent call to return. He declined. Farel again intervened, and Calvin found himself once more in Geneva, of which he was heard to have said, "There is no place under heaven of which I have greater dread." It was there that he labored under almost unimaginable conditions, and where for the majority of his adult life he was not granted citizenship but was made to feel, in every way, that he was but a pilgrim passing through.

At one point, he wrote a letter to the English refugees in Zurich explaining that there was much sorrow in being banished from one's home country. But there is another side: "Yet for the children of God, who know that they are the heirs of this world, it is not so difficult to be banished. It is in fact even good for them, so that through such an experience they can train themselves in being strangers on this earth."[6]

PHYSICAL AND EMOTIONAL SUFFERING

A second factor that contributed immensely to Calvin's longing for resurrection and heaven, and makes him a wise and faithful guide for us, was his physical and emotional suffering. His physical health was aggravated by working late into the night and waking up at 4 A.M. each day. Added to this was the stress he faced daily from pastoral duties, a lack of exercise, too much work, and relentless insomnia.

Calvin's afflictions read like a medical journal.[7] He suffered throughout his adult life from painful stomach cramps and recurring digestive problems, intestinal influenza, and constant migraine headaches. He was subject to a persistent onslaught of fevers that would often lay him up for weeks at a time. He experienced problems with his trachea in addition to pleurisy, gout, and colic. He suffered from hemorrhoids that were often aggravated by an internal abscess that would not heal. He had severe arthritis and acute pain in his knees, calves, and feet. Other maladies included nephritis (acute, chronic inflammation of the kidney caused by infection), gallstones, malaria, and kidney stones. He once passed a kidney stone so large that it tore the urinary canal and led to excessive bleeding.

Due to his rigorous preaching schedule (he preached twice on Sunday and every day of the week, every other week), he would often strain his voice so severely that he experienced violent fits of coughing. On one occasion, he broke a blood vessel in his lungs and hemorrhaged. When he reached the age of fifty-one, it was discovered that he was suffering from pulmonary tuberculosis, which ultimately proved fatal. Much of his study and writing was done while bedridden. In the final few years of his life, he had to be carried to work.

There is simply no way to read Calvin's comments on the glory of heaven and the passionate intensity of his longing for entrance into that

---

[6]Selderhuis, *John Calvin*, 83.
[7]The following description is adapted from my book *Chosen for Life: The Case for Divine Election* (Wheaton, IL: Crossway, 2007), 46–52.

phase of eternal life and not recognize how it was largely shaped by the daily agonies and anguish that he endured while a pastor in Geneva.[8]

WHY HEAVEN WILL BE HEAVENLY

The third reason why Calvin is so helpful to us in cultivating a passion for heaven was his vision and understanding of Jesus as the reason why heaven will be heavenly. If Calvin longed for the resurrection and glorification of the body only, or even primarily, to escape the manifold agonies that he suffered throughout the course of his life, he would not be for us the faithful guide that he is. If Calvin wrote of heaven and spoke of its glory only or primarily because there, in the new heavens and new earth, he would find a permanent and eternal residence, he would be unworthy of our attention. What made heaven heavenly for Calvin was Christ!

Calvin was deeply moved by Paul's declaration that "our citizenship is in heaven, and from it we await a Savior, the Lord Jesus Christ, who will transform our lowly body to be like his glorious body" (Phil. 3:20–21). Therefore, wrote Calvin, "as Christ is in heaven, in order that we may be conjoined with him, it is necessary that we should in spirit dwell apart from this world. . . . Christ, who is our blessedness and glory, is in heaven; let our souls, therefore, dwell with him on high."[9] Again, it was not primarily his anticipation of his "lowly" body being transformed that stirred his heart to look forward to the resurrection and the new heavens and new earth, but rather that "in heaven" we find Christ! *Christ*, who is our blessedness and glory, is in heaven. Let our souls, therefore, dwell with *him* on high.

In a similar vein, Calvin had much to say about our Lord's prayer in John 17:24—"Father, I desire that they also, whom you have given me, may be with me where I am, to see my glory that you have given me

---

[8]The weakness and persistent frailty of his own physical constitution must have influenced Calvin's belief that nothing is more at variance with human reason than the notion that our bodies will be raised up and glorified on the last day. "For who but God alone could persuade us that bodies, which are now liable to corruption, will, after having rotted away, or after they have been consumed by fire, or torn in pieces by wild beasts, will not merely be restored entire, but in a greatly better condition. Do not all our apprehensions of things straightway reject this as a thing fabulous, nay, most absurd?" (*Commentary on the Epistles of Paul the Apostle to the Corinthians,* trans. Rev. John Pringle [Grand Rapids, MI: Baker Book House, 2005], 20:46, commenting on 1 Cor. 15:35. Therefore, "we must not here form our judgment according to our own understanding, but must assign to the stupendous and secret power of God the honour of believing, that it will accomplish what we cannot comprehend" (ibid., 47).

[9]Calvin, *Commentaries on the Epistles of Paul the Apostle to the Philippians, Colossians, and Thessalonians,* 21:109.

because you loved me before the foundation of the world." In this passage, Calvin writes,

> Christ speaks of the perfect happiness of believers, as if he had said, that his desire will not be satisfied till they have been received into heaven. In the same manner I explain the *beholding of the glory*. At that time they saw the *glory* of Christ, just as a man shut up in the dark obtains, through small chinks, a feeble and glimmering light. Christ now wishes that they shall make such progress as to enjoy the full brightness of heaven. In short, he asks that the Father will conduct them, by uninterrupted progress, to the full vision of his *glory*.[10]

Thus to "enjoy the full brightness of heaven" is to see and savor God in all his glory! Indeed, "if God contains the fullness of all good things in himself like an inexhaustible fountain, nothing beyond him is to be sought by those who strive after the highest good and all the elements of happiness, as we are taught in many passages."[11]

MEDITATING ON HEAVEN

Fourth, Calvin is exceptionally helpful to us because of the way he instructs us to *meditate* on heaven and the final resurrection. Could it be that the indescribably practical, productive, and life-changing value of his labors and all that he accomplished during his earthly sojourn were due to his incessant and focused meditation on heaven? Yes!

There are several places in his commentaries on the New Testament where we see this emphasis. In Romans 8:23, Paul speaks of the inward "groaning" of both the natural creation and the children of God to enter into the fullness of our heavenly reward. Paul's point, wrote Calvin, is this:

> The excellency of our glory is of such importance even to the very elements, which are destitute of mind and reason, that they burn with a certain kind of desire for it; how much more it behooves us, who have been illuminated by the Spirit of God, to aspire and strive with firmness of hope and with ardour of desire, after the attainment of so great a benefit.[12]

---

[10] John Calvin, *Commentary on the Gospel According to John* (Grand Rapids, MI: Baker Books, 2005), 187.
[11] John Calvin, *Institutes of the Christian Religion*, ed. John T. McNeill, trans. Ford Lewis Battl. (Philadelphia, PA: The Westminster Press, 1975), 3.25.10.
[12] John Calvin, *Commentaries on the Epistle of Paul the Apostle to the Romans* (Grand Rapids, MI: Baker Book House, 2005), 308.

Speaking once again in the light of Philippians 3:21 and the transformation of our bodies, Paul stirs us up to lift our minds to heaven,

> because this body which we carry about with us is not an everlasting abode, but a frail tabernacle, which will in short time be reduced to nothing. Besides, it is liable to so many miseries, and so many dishonourable infirmities, that it may justly be spoken of as *vile* and full of ignomity. Whence, then, is its restoration to be hoped for? From heaven, at Christ's coming. *Hence there is no part of us that ought not to aspire after heaven with undivided affection.*[13]

In his commentary on 1 Peter 1:9, Calvin highlights how "the Apostle sets before us this future life as a subject of deep meditation."[14] To allow our souls "to grovel on the earth would be inconsistent and unworthy of those whose *treasure is in heaven.*"[15] Again, commenting on 1 Peter 1:4, he contends that the apostles' words are designed "to impress our minds thoroughly as to its [heaven's] excellency."[16] And what is the "excellency" of heaven? Peter mentions three things.

Our heavenly inheritance, says Peter, is *imperishable.* One thing that makes life so hard now is that virtually everything we love and cherish and trust ultimately dies. Our bodies decay and die. Our friends and family decay and die. The animal kingdom decays and dies. Plants and flowers and the beauty of nature ultimately decay and die. But the glory and splendor of life in the new heavens and new earth will never decay or die. No disintegration. No dissolution. Constantly and forever renewed and refreshed. Always and ever alive. Always and ever vibrant. Always and ever fresh and new.

Our heavenly inheritance is *undefiled.* No matter how much we try in the present day to keep things clean, they get dirty. We buy detergent and spot remover and cleansing agents and soap and disinfectants of every conceivable sort. Yet all that we see and touch and taste and own suffers defilement and is subject to impurity, both physically and morally. But not on the new earth! Nothing in that place of glory will ever be anything but pristine and pure and clean and devoid of spot or wrinkle.

---

[13]Calvin, *Commentaries on the Epistles of Paul the Apostle to the Philippians, Colossians, and Thessalonians,* 110 (emphasis mine).
[14]Calvin, *Commentaries on the Catholic Epistles,* 36.
[15]John Calvin, *Commentary on a Harmony of the Evangelists, Matthew, Mark, and Luke* (Grand Rapids, MI: Baker Books, 2005), 334 (emphasis mine).
[16]Calvin, *Commentaries on the Catholic Epistles,* 29.

Finally, this inheritance is *unfading*. Everything now is subject to the ravages of time. All creation is breaking down and losing its luster. All beauty now is fast fading away. Not all the tummy tucks or face-lifts or Botox or plastic surgery in the world can slow down the steady onslaught of time and age. The most beautiful sculptures eventually wear away. The colors and hues in the most beautiful paintings eventually lose their brilliance. But not on the new earth! Nothing there will ever get old or ugly or become outdated or obsolete. With each passing moment in the new heavens and new earth, there will be new colors and new sounds and new discoveries of the beauty of God. Our inheritance, unlike every possession and experience in this life, will never lose its capacity to bring happiness and joy, to enthrall and excite.

This, says Calvin, is the "excellency" of heaven. This is the living hope to which you have been born again because Jesus was raised from the dead. And in this, says Peter, you find great and deep and lasting joy. In this you find strength to endure trials and setbacks and disappointments. In this, says Peter, you find hope when everything else is hopeless. This glorious truth is what will sustain and empower you for everything that lies ahead.

THE PRACTICAL POWER OF MEDITATING ON THE HEAVENLY LIFE

Unlike Jonathan Edwards, Calvin did not make an effort to provide us with an extended or detailed description of the beauty of heaven and all that awaits the believer.[17] There is nothing in Calvin's writings comparable to Edwards's *Heaven, A World of Love*. But equally, if not more so than Edwards, Calvin spoke and wrote and preached often of the way in which the reality and certainty of heaven affects and empowers us now. For Calvin, as much as for anyone I have ever encountered or read, the certainty of the future impinges on and invades the circumstances of the present.

Let's now direct our attention to what Calvin had to say on the practical benefits of meditating on heaven. I would like us to think together and

---

[17]He did, however, speak of the eternal happiness of the final resurrection and heaven as "a happiness of whose excellence the minutest part would scarce be told if all were said that the tongues of all men can say. For though we very truly hear that the Kingdom of God will be filled with splendor, joy, happiness, and glory, yet when these things are spoken of, they remain utterly remote from our perception, and, as it were, wrapped in obscurities, until that day comes when he will reveal to us his glory, that we may behold it face to face" (*Institutes*, 3.25.10).

be inspired and energized by what Calvin had to say concerning the manifold ways in which being "heavenly minded" is the pathway to becoming of profound "earthly good." We begin by looking at 2 Corinthians 4:16–18 and Calvin's observations on this remarkable text.

CALVIN AND 2 CORINTHIANS 4:16–18[18]

Paul's comments in 2 Corinthians 4:16–18 have in view the experience he described in verses 8–12—an experience that entails affliction, perplexity, persecution, and being struck down. What that meant for Paul and his ministry in Corinth might not be the same for you and me, but all of us, including Calvin, perhaps especially Calvin, face disappointment and suffering that threaten us with discouragement. So how does one not "lose heart," to use Paul's words? Where does one find the power to persevere? Here is what the apostle said:

> So we do not lose heart. Though our outer nature is wasting away, our inner nature is being renewed day by day. For this light momentary affliction is preparing for us an eternal weight of glory beyond all comparison, as we look not to the things that are seen but to the things that are unseen. For the things that are seen are transient, but the things that are unseen are eternal. (2 Cor. 4:16–18)

The *outer nature* in verse 16 is not a reference to the *old man* of Romans 6:6 (or Col. 3:9 or Eph. 4:22). The *old man* refers to the moral or ethical dimension of our fallen, unregenerate nature. *Outer nature*, on the other hand, refers to our bodily frame, our physical constitution, our creaturely mortality, the "jars of clay" or "earthen vessels" of 2 Corinthians 4:7. Therefore, the "decaying" or "wasting away" of our "outer nature" is most likely a reference once more to the hardships of verses 8–9, and our carrying about in our bodies the dying in Jesus of verse 10, and our being handed over to death in verse 11, and the death that is at work in us in verse 12. The "renewal" of the "inner nature," therefore, is probably synonymous with what Paul earlier said in 3:18 when he declared that "we . . . are being transformed into the same image from one degree of glory to another." By the "outward man," Calvin believes that Paul intends "everything that relates to the present life," such as "riches,

---

[18]Some of what follows has been adapted from my book *A Sincere and Pure Devotion to Christ: 100 Daily Meditations on 2 Corinthians* (Crossway, 2010).

honours, friendships, and other resources," as well as the physical body. Our outward man is being corrupted anytime we "suffer a diminution or loss of these blessings."[19]

As you might expect from Calvin, he argues that because we are "too much taken up with the present life,"[20] it is God himself who is responsible for this "wasting away" of the outer man. By orchestrating our lives in this way, God "calls us back to meditate on a better life."[21] It is, therefore, "necessary," said Calvin, not fortuitous or simply bad luck, but "necessary" by God's design "that the condition of the present life should decay."[22] It is necessary, says Calvin, "in order that the inward man may be in a flourishing state; because, in proportion as the *earthly* life declines, does the *heavenly* life advance, at least in believers."[23]

What does that tell us about our response to hardship and affliction and deprivation and suffering? If Calvin is right in his interpretation of Paul, and I think he is, it tells us that if we want our "heavenly life" to advance and to be as glorious and deeply satisfying as it possibly can be, it is necessary that our "earthly life declines."

Paul explains this in greater detail in verse 17. There he says, in utterly stunning terms, that the persecution he endures and the trials he confronts daily are but "light momentary affliction"! Paul was no Pollyanna. The suffering in his life was very real, not imaginary, and if viewed only from an earthly or temporal perspective would probably be, more than any human might endure. But when viewed through the eye of faith and from the vantage point of eternity, a new vantage is attained, and suffering is seen in an altogether different light.

Note carefully the contrasts in view: "momentary" is contrasted with "eternal," "light" is set over against "weight," and "affliction" is counterbalanced by "glory." Similar language is used by Paul in Romans 8:18, where he says that "the sufferings of this present time are not worth comparing with the glory that is to be revealed to us." Calvin was quick to point out that since we can only see the outward decay but not the inward renovation, "Paul, with the view of shaking us off from a carnal attachment to the present life, draws a comparison between present miseries

---

[19]Calvin, *Commentary on the Epistles of Paul the Apostle to the Corinthians*, 211.
[20]Ibid.
[21]Ibid.
[22]Ibid.
[23]Ibid.

and future felicity."[24] Because we so naturally tend to recoil from suffering and loss of comfort, "Paul on that account admonishes us, that the afflictions and vexations of the pious have little or nothing of bitterness, if compared with the boundless blessings of everlasting glory."[25] The apostle, therefore, "prescribes the best antidote against your sinking down under the pressure of afflictions, when he places in opposition to them that future blessedness which is *laid up for thee in heaven* (Col. 1:5)."[26]

What Calvin called "the common miseries of mankind" are, he says, "a blessing from God" because they prepare us "for a blessed resurrection."[27] And the only way to endure and profit from such miseries is "if we carry forward our thoughts to the eternity of the heavenly kingdom."[28] God is not asking us to treat pain as though it were pleasure, or grief as though it were joy, but to bring all earthly adversity into comparison with heavenly glory and thereby be strengthened to endure. It is encouraging to know that whatever suffering we might endure now, in this age characterized by pain and injustice, cannot overturn or undermine the purposes of God!

But note well. This inner transformation in the midst of outer decay does not happen automatically. Carefully observe the relation between verse 16 and verse 18. The renewal Paul describes (verse 16) only occurs while or to the extent that "we look not to the things that are seen but to the things that are unseen. For the things that are seen are transient, but the things that are unseen are eternal" (verse 18). As we fix the gaze of our hearts on the glorious hope of the age to come, God progressively renews our inner beings, notwithstanding the simultaneous decay of our outer beings! Note also that this is no fleeting or casual glance or occasional thought concerning the "glory" of the age to come. The apostle has in mind a fixity of gaze, an attentive and studious concentration on the inestimable blessings of heaven. The contrast between "the things that are seen" and "the things that are unseen" has in view the distinction between the present age and all that is temporal and subject to sin and decay, as over against the unchanging righteousness and incorruptible reality of the age to come.

We must never use this passage to justify a careless, indifferent, or

---

[24]Ibid., 212.
[25]Ibid.
[26]Ibid.
[27]Ibid., 213.
[28]Ibid., 214.

neglectful disregard for the daily responsibilities of life in the present day. Paul is simply warning us against a carnal fixation on what this world system can provide and calling us to set our hope and confidence on the eternal values of God's kingdom. Here, then, is the power to persevere: by setting your mind and fixing your gaze and focusing your heart on the unseen yet eternal realities of what God has secured for you in Christ.

So how does this actually work in daily experience? If we follow Paul's counsel, what difference does it make now, amidst the struggles and disappointments and pain of earthly life? Here is where Calvin is so immensely helpful. As I earlier cited four reasons why Calvin is a competent guide for us as we think of the final resurrection and heaven, let me now mention four practical benefits identified by Calvin that come to us from looking "not to the things that are seen but to the things that are unseen." So here we have *the practical, life-changing, sin-killing, hope-inspiring effect of meditating on the glories of heaven and the life to come.*

ENDURING UNJUST SUFFERING

First, contemplating the splendor of heaven empowers the believer to patiently endure unjust suffering. Calvin's life was in some ways an unending, torturous ordeal in which he was subjected to slander, reproach, vilification, hatred, taunting, incessant resistance to his proposals, and public mockery of his attempts to proclaim the gospel and pastor the people of Geneva. Perhaps nothing exacted a greater toll on his spirit and body than the aftermath of the execution of Michael Servetus. Many believe it contributed to his early death. In a letter to Johannes Wolf, we get a sense for the devastating effect it had on him. He wrote this on Christmas Day in 1555 when he was only forty-six years old.

> Believe me, I had fewer troubles with Servetus . . . than I have with those who are close at hand, whose numbers are beyond reckoning and whose passions are irreconcilable. If one could choose, it would be better to be burned once by the papists than to be plagued for eternity by one's neighbours. They do not allow me a moment's rest, although they can clearly see that I am collapsing under the burden of work, troubled by endless sad occurrences, and disturbed by intrusive demands. My one comfort is that death will soon take me from this all too difficult service.[29]

---

[29]Cited in Bruce Gordon, *Calvin* (New Haven, CT, and London: Yale University Press, 2009), 233. Letter to Johannes Wolf, 25 December, 1555. Rudolf Schwarz, ed., *Johannes Calvins Lebenswerk in seinen Briefen* (Tübingen: J. C. B. Mohr, 1909), 2:118–119).

As we consider his observations on the many biblical texts that address this theme, we must not think for a moment that Calvin writes as a detached and distant observer, as if he were only concerned with the academic accuracy of his interpretations. These passages were his very life. They sustained him and gave him hope.

Consider Jesus' encouragement in Matthew 5:12 where he responds to the reality of persecution and slander against those who follow him: "Rejoice and be glad, for your reward is great in heaven." The meaning, said Calvin, is that "a remedy is at hand, that we may not be overwhelmed by unjust reproaches: for, as soon as we raise our minds to heaven, we there behold vast grounds of joy, which dispel sadness."[30] Calvin never suggests, as do the purveyors of health, wealth, and the power of positive thinking, that if we but "raise our minds to heaven" all such pain and persecution will disappear. No, but there, in the midst of unending pain and persecution, we "behold vast grounds of joy, which dispel sadness."

Calvin must have resonated in an unusually personal and vivid way with Paul's language in Romans 8:23, where the apostle speaks of "groaning" in anticipation of the redemption of our bodies. Don't merely listen to Calvin the commentator. Hear the heart of a suffering man whose grip was strengthened by the promise of resurrection:

> [Paul] requires that there should be a feeling of two kinds in the faithful: that being burdened with the sense of their present misery, they are to *groan*; and that notwithstanding they are to *wait* patiently for their deliverance [both groaning and waiting]; for he would have them to be raised up with the expectation of their future blessedness, and by an elevation of mind to overcome all their present miseries, while they consider not what they are now, but what they are to be.[31]

Note again: It is by "an elevation of mind" to contemplate your "future blessedness" that you can overcome all your "present miseries." He says much the same thing in view of Paul's comments in Romans 8:25.

---

[30]Calvin, *Commentary on a Harmony of the Evangelists, Matthew, Mark, and Luke*, 267. In the prefatory statement where he surveys the argument of Romans, Calvin comments on Paul's words in Romans 8. "He further shows, for the purpose of anticipating objections, that the certainty of eternal life cannot be intercepted or disturbed by present evils, to which we are subject in this life; but that, on the contrary, our salvation is promoted by such trials, and that the value of it, when compared with our present miseries, renders them as nothing" (*Commentaries on the Epistle of Paul the Apostle to the Romans*, xxxiv).
[31]Ibid., 308.

It may be added, that we have here a remarkable passage, which shows, that patience is an inseparable companion of faith; and the reason of this is evident, for when we console ourselves with the hope of a better condition, the feeling of our present miseries is softened and mitigated, so that they are borne with less difficulty.[32]

Merely being aware of how bad things are in the present and speaking at length of the pain they inflict does nothing to help us persevere. In 2 Corinthians 5:1, the apostle reminds us that notwithstanding the decay and destruction of our earthly bodies we have "a building from God, a house not made with hands, eternal in the heavens." It is not enough, says Calvin, "to be aware of the miseries of this life."[33] That will only serve to create a morbid and sullen existence. He insists that at the same time we must have in view "the felicity and glory of the future life." It is thinking often and deeply of "the supreme and perfect blessedness, which awaits believers in heaven after death" that empowers us to endure.[34]

We find much the same emphasis in his comments on 1 John 3:2 where we are assured of being conformed to the image of Christ. Our bodies are but dust and a shadow, and death is ever before our eyes. We are, said Calvin, "subject to [a] thousand miseries, and the soul is exposed to innumerable evils; so that we find always a hell within us."[35] This is what makes it necessary to turn our thoughts from the present, lest "the miseries by which we are on every side surrounded and almost overwhelmed, should shake our faith in that felicity which as yet lies hid."[36]

Nowhere does Calvin say it with more passion and energy than in his *Institutes*. There you can hear the echo of his own suffering and the heaviness of the constant reproach that he endured, yet also through it all is the hope of heaven that sustained him.

To the huge mass of miseries that almost overwhelms us are added the jests of profane men, which assail our innocence when we, willingly renouncing the allurements of present benefits, seem to strive after a blessedness hidden from us as if it were a fleeing shadow. Finally,

---

[32]Ibid., 310.
[33]Calvin, *Commentary on the Epistles of Paul the Apostle to the Corinthians*, 216.
[34]Ibid.
[35]Calvin, *Commentaries on the Catholic Epistles*, 204.
[36]Ibid. "For in heaven is our felicity, and we are now far away traveling on the earth; for this fading life, constantly exposed to hundred deaths, is far different from that eternal life which belongs to the children of God; for being enclosed as slaves in the prison of our flesh, we are far distant from the full sovereignty of heaven and earth" (ibid.).

above and below us, before us and behind, violent temptations besiege us, which our minds would be quite unable to sustain, were they not freed of earthly things and bound to the heavenly life, which appears to be far away. Accordingly, he alone has fully profited in the gospel who has accustomed himself to continual meditation upon the blessed resurrection.[37]

OVERCOMING THE SNARES

Second, meditating on the beauty of heaven strengthens the soul to overcome the snares of this life. Let me simply cite several of Calvin's statements on this point so that you might feel the cumulative impact of how his own contemplation of heavenly glory strengthened him in the battle.

They are said to do so [i.e., to lay up for themselves treasures in heaven], who, instead of entangling themselves in the snares of this world, make it their care and their business to meditate on the heavenly life.[38]

But if we were honestly and firmly convinced that our happiness is in heaven, it would be easy for us to trample upon the world, to despise earthly blessings, (by the deceitful attractions of which the greater part of men are fascinated,) and to rise towards heaven.[39]

If meditation on the heavenly life were the prevailing sentiment in our hearts, the world would have no influence in detaining us.[40]

The lusts of the flesh hold us entangled, when in our minds we dwell in the world, and think not that heaven is our country; but when we pass as strangers through this life, we are not in bondage to the flesh.[41]

The apostle John stated in 1 John 3:3 that "everyone who thus hopes in him [i.e., in Christ] purifies himself as he is pure." The meaning of this, says Calvin, is "that though we have not Christ now present before our eyes, yet if we hope in him, it cannot be but that this hope will excite and stimulate us to follow purity, for it leads us straight to Christ, whom we

---

[37]*Institutes*, 3.25.1.
[38]Calvin, *Commentary on a Harmony of the Evangelists, Matthew, Mark, and Luke*, 332.
[39]Ibid., 334.
[40]Calvin, *Commentary on the Gospel According to John*, 30.
[41]Calvin, *Commentaries on the Catholic Epistles*, 78.

know to be a perfect pattern of purity."[42] Although Calvin would never
have endorsed the last days madness so prevalent not long ago in our
Western world, he asks, "For whence is it that flesh indulges itself except
that there is no thought of the near coming of Christ?"[43]

Perhaps Calvin's greatest insights in this regard are found in his
commentary on 1 Corinthians 15:58. Paul's exhortation is that we "be
steadfast, immovable, always abounding in the work of the Lord, knowing that in the Lord your labor is not in vain." How do we know that
our labor is not in vain? Because there is a reward laid up for us with
God. This is the hope, says Calvin, that "encourages believers, and afterward sustains them, so that they do not stop short in the race."[44] The
Pauline exhortation to remain steadfast is based on the sure foundation
that "a better life is prepared" for us "in heaven."[45] It is "the hope of a
resurrection [that] makes us not be weary in well-doing."[46] In the face
of so many temptations to quit and fall into despair, our only hope, says
Calvin, is "by thinking of a better life."[47] Indeed, "if the hope of a resurrection is taken away, then, the foundation (as it were) being rooted up,
the whole structure of piety falls to the ground. Unquestionably, if the
hope of reward is taken away and extinguished, alacrity in running will
not merely grow cold, but will be altogether destroyed."[48]

RESPONDING RIGHTLY TO DEATH

Third, thinking often of heaven and the age to come, not only enables
us to hold onto this life loosely, but also helps us to respond properly to
the death of others and to be prepared for our own departure. We need
to begin with the clear understanding that as much as Calvin spoke of
longing for death, *he never despised life.* He regarded it as an indescribably immense blessing from God. One need only observe how incredibly
productive he was during his short time on earth. But what of our Lord's
statement in John 12:25 that we are to "hate" life in this world?

Jesus does not mean, says Calvin, that we are "absolutely to *hate life*,
which is justly reckoned to be one of the highest of God's blessings."[49]

---

[42]Ibid., 207.
[43]Ibid., 420.
[44]Calvin, *Commentary on the Epistles of Paul the Apostle to the Corinthians*, 66.
[45]Ibid.
[46]Ibid.
[47]Ibid.
[48]Ibid.
[49]Calvin, *Commentary on the Gospel According to John*, 29.

Rather, we should "cheerfully" lay it down when it hinders us from coming to Christ.[50] In other words, "to love this life is not in itself wrong, provided that we only pass through it as pilgrims, keeping our eyes always fixed on our object."[51] We "hate" this life only to the extent that it hinders or inhibits or detracts from our intimacy with Jesus. Jesus thus speaks of hating this life "to strike terror into those who are too desirous of the earthly life; for if we are overwhelmed by the love of the world, so that we cannot easily forget it, it is impossible for us to go to heaven."[52]

We also must reckon with the pointed and sometimes painful way in which Calvin spoke of how God uses trials and sufferings and tragedies in this life to wean us from excessive dependence upon the present and to turn our attention to heaven. Indeed, "since God knows best how much we are inclined by nature to a brutish love of this world, he uses the fittest means to draw us back and to shake off our sluggishness, lest we cleave too tenaciously to that love."[53]

Why do we not aspire more passionately to the heavenly life? "Now our blockishness arises from the fact that our minds, stunned by the empty dazzlement of riches, power, and honors, become so deadened that they can see no farther."[54] And therefore, "to counter this evil the Lord instructs his followers in the vanity of the present life by continual proof of its miseries."[55]

Here Calvin's robust belief in the absolute sovereignty of God over all of life permeates his thought. Lest we be seduced by "peace," God permits wars and robbery and other "injuries."[56] Lest we be seduced by riches, he sometimes "reduces them to poverty, or at least confines them to a moderate station."[57] Lest we become complacent in the benefits of marriage, God "either causes them to be troubled by the depravity of their wives or humbles them by evil offspring, or afflicts them with bereavement."[58] We conclude from this "that in this life we are to seek and hope for nothing but struggle; when we think of our crown, we are to raise our eyes to heaven. For this we must believe: that the mind is

---

[50]Ibid.
[51]Ibid.
[52]Ibid., 30.
[53]*Institutes*, 3.9.1.
[54]Ibid.
[55]Ibid.
[56]Ibid.
[57]Ibid.
[58]Ibid.

never seriously aroused to desire and ponder the life to come unless it be previously imbued with contempt for the present life."[59]

When Calvin speaks, as often he does, about this life as one that should be "despised and trampled under foot,"[60] it is only the result of having compared it with the heavenly life to come. We only hate this present life "in so far as it holds us subject to sin."[61] There should be no "murmuring and impatience"[62] should God choose to leave us here for a while.

Calvin reserved some of his most pointed observations on death and our attitudes toward it in his commentary on 2 Corinthians 5. The wicked and unbelieving cling to life and view death with horror. "The *groaning* of believers, on the other hand, arises from this—that they know, that they are here in a state of exile from their native land, and that they know, that they are here shut up in the body as in a prison. Hence they feel this life to be a *burden,* because in it they cannot enjoy true and perfect blessedness, because they cannot escape from the bondage of sin otherwise than by death, and hence they aspire to be elsewhere."[63]

There is nothing sinfully morbid in longing for death, says Calvin, because *"believers do not desire death for the sake of losing any thing, but as having regard to a better life."*[64] The way we overcome the natural fear of death is by thinking of it as the discarding of a "coarse," "dirty," "tattered" garment, all with a view toward "being arrayed in an elegant, handsome, new, and durable one."[65] Christians should not break down "under the severity of the cross" or be "disheartened by afflictions," says Calvin. In fact, such experiences ought to make us even more courageous. We "long" for death, not from a perverse desire for pain but because it is "the commencement of perfect blessedness."[66] And again:

> For nothing is better than to quit the body, that we may attain near intercourse with God, and may truly and openly enjoy his presence. Hence by the decay of the body we lose nothing that belongs to us.
>
> Observe here—what has been once stated already—that true faith begets not merely a contempt of death, but even a desire for it, and that

[59]Ibid.
[60]*Institutes,* 3.9.4.
[61]Ibid.
[62]Ibid.
[63]Calvin, *Commentary on the Epistles of Paul the Apostle to the Corinthians,* 218–219.
[64]Ibid., 219.
[65]Ibid.
[66]Ibid., 222.

it is, accordingly, on the other hand, a token of unbelief, when dread of death predominates in us above the joy and consolation of hope.[67]

Calvin speaks very boldly on this point, arguing that *one of the clearest indications of a false faith is the lingering fear of death*:

> In the mean time, believers do not cease to regard death with horror, but when they turn their eyes to that life which follows death, they easily overcome all dread by means of that consolation. Unquestionably, every one that believes in Christ ought to be so courageous as to *lift up his head* on mention being made of death, delighted to have intimation of his *redemption* (Luke xxi.28). From this we see how many are Christians only in name, since the greater part, on hearing mention made of death, are not merely alarmed, but are rendered almost lifeless through fear, as though they had never heard a single word respecting Christ.[68]

Fixing our eyes on heaven helps us overcome the fear of death by producing hope.

> There is, however, an implied contrast between the present condition in which believers labour and groan, and that final restoration. For they are *now* exposed to the reproaches of the world, and are looked upon as vile and worthless; but *then* they will be precious, and full of dignity, when Christ will pour forth his glory upon them. The end of this is, that the pious may as it were, with closed eyes, pursue the brief journey of this earthly life, having their minds always intent upon the future manifestation of Christ's kingdom. For to what purpose does he make mention of his coming in power, but in order that they may in hope leap forward to that blessed resurrection which is as yet hid?[69]

As noted earlier, a proper perspective on the certainty of resurrection and the beauty of heaven will keep us from excessively mourning the death of other believers. This was Paul's point in 1 Thessalonians 4:13 where he warned us against grieving "as others do who have no hope." We must not "bewail the dead beyond due bounds," said Calvin, "inasmuch as we are all to be raised up again."[70] It is unbecoming for a

---

[67]Ibid.
[68]Calvin, *Commentaries on the Epistles of Paul the Apostle to the Philippians, Colossians, and Thessalonians*, 43–44.
[69]Ibid., 319.
[70]Ibid., 279.

Christian "to mourn otherwise than in moderation."[71] Indeed, it is "the knowledge of a resurrection," says Calvin, that serves as "the means of moderating grief."[72] Calvin is not recommending stoical indifference toward the reality of death and the departure of our loved ones. It is "one thing to bridle our grief, that it may be subject to God, and quite another thing to harden one's self so as to be like stones, by casting away human feelings. Let, therefore, the grief of the pious be mixed with consolation, which may train them to patience. The hope of a blessed resurrection, which is the mother of patience, will effect this."[73]

In any case, since we both live and die unto the Lord, let it be in such a way that we "burn with the zeal for death and be constant in meditation."[74] It is in fact "monstrous"[75] that Christians should ever be gripped by a fear of death. Indeed, "let us . . . consider this settled: that no one has made progress in the school of Christ who does not joyfully await the day of death and final resurrection."[76]

RESPONDING WELL TO LOSS

Fourth and finally, setting our hearts on heaven enables us to respond well to the loss of money and property in this present life. Although there were seasons in Calvin's early life when he struggled financially to make ends meet, he rarely if ever gave any indication of avarice or resentment or bitterness. Toward the end of life and ministry in Geneva, he was paid well but never became presumptuous or dependent on earthly comforts. Bruce Gordon argues that "his sermons reveal a man whose attitudes towards material things were far more interesting and textured than his reputation suggests."[77] He enjoyed good wine, good conversation with friends, good music, and good art. But he never trusted in them.

Calvin's perspective is best seen in his comments on Hebrews 10:34. There we read, "For you had compassion on those in prison, and you joyfully accepted the plundering of your property, since you knew that you yourselves had a better possession and an abiding one." Calvin is quick to

---

[71]Ibid. Thus Paul's point in this passage was "simply to restrain excessive grief, which would never have had such an influence among them, if they had seriously considered the resurrection, and kept it in remembrance" (ibid.).
[72]Ibid.
[73]Ibid., 280.
[74]*Institutes*, 3.9.4.
[75]*Institutes*, 3.9.5.
[76]*Institutes*, 3.9.5.
[77]Gordon, *Calvin*, 147.

point out that these people had feelings and that the loss of their property undoubtedly caused them grief, but not to such an extent that all joy was taken. "As poverty is deemed an evil, the plunder of their goods considered in itself touched them with grief; but as they looked higher, they found a cause for joy, which allayed whatever grief they felt. It is indeed thus necessary that our thoughts should be drawn away from the world, by looking at the heavenly recompense."[78] Whatever pain they endured, such "feelings never so prevail in overwhelming them with grief, but that with their minds raised up to heaven they emerge into spiritual joy."[79] Because "their minds were fixed on the recompense, they easily forgot the grief occasioned by their present calamity. And indeed wherever there is a lively perception of heavenly things, the world with all its allurements is not so relished, that either poverty or shame can overwhelm our minds with grief. If then we wish to bear anything for Christ with patience and resigned minds, let us accustom ourselves to a frequent meditation on that felicity, in comparison with which all the good things of the world are nothing but refuse."[80]

WITH ONE FOOT RAISED

In closing, let us return briefly to where we began, with Calvin's pastoral counsel to Madame de Coligny: "We ought to learn to have *one foot raised* to take our departure when it shall please God." Were he with us today, I suspect his advice would remain unchanged.

Young man, young woman, go to school, study hard, prepare yourself for fifty or more years in a productive and exciting career. But do it with one foot raised!

Let all of us diligently labor at our place of business. Honor our employers by giving them a good day's work for a day's wage. But always work with one foot raised!

By all means, get married. Enjoy the delight of romantic affections. Devote yourself to your spouse, yet do it with one foot raised!

Be quick to educate your children. Prepare them for life. Raise them in the nurture and admonition of the Lord, but always with one foot raised!

Study Greek and Hebrew and Latin! But study with one foot raised!

---

[78]John Calvin, *Commentaries on the Epistle of Paul the Apostle to the Hebrews*, 254.
[79]Ibid.
[80]Ibid., 255.

Celebrate life with your friends over a good steak and your beverage of choice. But eat and drink with one foot raised!

Weep at the grave site of a child. Mourn at the loss of a friend. But may it always be with one foot raised!

Read a book. Write a book. But read and write with one foot raised!

Cheer for your favorite football team and celebrate wildly with every victory. But do it with one foot raised!

Labor to enact legislation to improve life in your city, your state, your country, but always with one foot raised!

Plant a garden. Plant a church. Open a savings account. Purchase a thirty-year certificate of deposit. Invest in a stock. But do it all in anticipation and heightened expectancy of the life to come. Do it all with one foot raised!

6

JESUS CHRIST AS DÉNOUEMENT IN THE THEATER OF GOD:

Calvin & the Supremacy of Christ in All Things

John Piper

The question I am trying to answer in this final chapter is how Jesus Christ relates to the ultimate purpose of God in the theater of God. You may see right away that this question contains several subquestions. What is the ultimate goal of God in the theater of God? How do the historical work and the eternal person of the Son of God relate to the ultimate goal of God in this theater? Is the created universe the theater of God? What difference does it make for us? And, of course, does John Calvin give us any help here?

DÉNOUEMENT

I had the happy fortune of being a literature major in college, so the word *dénouement* is in my vocabulary. It may not be in yours. The dictionary says that the *dénouement* is "the final part of a play, movie, or narrative in which the strands of the plot are drawn together and matters are explained or resolved." Or: "the climax of a chain of events, usually when something is decided or made clear." So I am taking it to mean roughly the climactic point where the goal of the drama reaches its decisive, but not necessarily final, expression.

And, of course, you might think it doesn't make sense to call a person the *dénouement*. The *dénouement* is an event. But what we are going to find out is that unlike everyone else in the universe, the work and the person of Jesus demand that we think of *dénouement* in unusual ways. More on that later.

ON CALVIN

Just a word about Calvin. Since I am sure he would want us to end with a focus not on Calvin but on his Christ, my aim in this message is to be expository—to show from biblical texts a portrait of Christ that is true and wonderful. My aim is not to interpret Calvin, but to make much of Jesus Christ.

At least two things have been burned on my mind with the help of John Calvin: the majesty of the Word of God—the Bible—and the supreme worth of the glory of God manifest above all in Jesus Christ.

A PASSION FOR THE GLORY OF CHRIST

His passion for the glory of Christ began at his conversion and grew for a lifetime. When he was thirty years old, he hoped that in the end he would be able to say,

> The thing [O God] at which I chiefly aimed, and for which I most dili-gently labored, was, that the glory of thy goodness and justice . . . might shine forth conspicuous, that the virtue and blessings of thy Christ . . . might be fully displayed.[1]

Here we have the language of God's glory "shining forth" and the worth of Christ being "fully displayed." This, he would say, is what the theater of God is for and therefore what his life was for: the shining forth of God's glory and the full display of the greatness of Christ.

GLORY TO CHRIST—IN JUSTIFICATION AND MARTYRDOM

When he wrestled with the Roman church over the doctrine of justifica-tion, the main issue was: "Wherever the knowledge of it [justification by faith alone] is taken away, the glory of Christ is extinguished."[2] The

---

[1]John Dillenberger, *John Calvin, Selections from His Writings* (Atlanta: American Academy of Religion, 1975), 110.
[2]Ibid., 95.

main issue was not our conscience or assurance. The main issue was this: If the imputation of the righteousness of Christ is denied, the glory of Christ is cut in half in the work of salvation.[3]

The glory of Christ was central not only in the matter of justification but also in the matter of martyrdom. As he did so often, Calvin wrote a letter to a group of women who had been imprisoned in France for their Reformed convictions, and the note he struck pastorally was the same one he struck doctrinally: "For this we were brought into the world and enlightened by God's grace, that we should magnify him in our life and our death."[4] Magnifying, displaying, making conspicuous the glory of Christ—that is the issue from justification to martyrdom.

D'Aubigné, the great historian of the nineteenth century, summed up Calvin's passion like this:

> All Calvin's life proclaimed, glory, glory, glory to Christ, and to self confusion of face. Glory to his *Word*, glory to his *person*, glory to his *grace*, glory to his *life*. These are the four "glories" which both the Apostle and Reformer invite you to render to the Lord.[5]

THE MAJESTY OF GOD'S WORD

Calvin would want me to join him in giving glory to Jesus in this last chapter, and he would want me to do it mainly with the Word of God, which is the second thing burned on my mind by John Calvin—the majesty of God's Word. I know this because he said,

> Let the pastors boldly dare all things by the word of God. . . . Let them constrain all the power, glory, and excellence of the world to give place to and to obey the divine majesty of this word. Let them enjoin everyone by it, from the highest to the lowest. Let them edify the body of Christ.

---

[3]Calvin writes, "[W]e simply interpret justification, as the acceptance with which God receives us into his favor as if we were righteous; and we say that this justification consists in the forgiveness of sins and the imputation of the righteousness of Christ." *Institutes*, 3.11.2. He continues, "[I]t is proved, that it is entirely by the intervention of Christ's righteousness that we obtain justification before God. This is equivalent to saying that man is not just in himself, but that the righteousness of Christ is communicated to him by imputation, while he is strictly deserving of punishment. Thus vanishes the absurd dogma, that man is justified by faith, inasmuch as it brings him under the influence of the Spirit of God by whom he is rendered righteous. . . . You see that our righteousness is not in ourselves, but in Christ; that the only way in which we become possessed of it is by being made partakers with Christ, since with him we possess all riches. . . . To declare that we are deemed righteous, solely because the obedience of Christ is imputed to us as if it were our own, is just to place our righteousness in the obedience of Christ." Ibid., 3.11.23.

[4]J. H. Merle d' Aubigné, *Let Christ Be Magnified: Calvin's Teaching for Today* (Edinburgh: Banner of Truth Trust, 2007), 9.

[5]Ibid.

Let them devastate Satan's reign. Let them pasture the sheep, kill the wolves, instruct and exhort the rebellious. Let them bind and loose thunder and lightning, if necessary, but let them do all according to the word of God.[6]

So we turn to our questions. What is the ultimate goal of God in the theater of God? How do the historical work and the eternal person of the Son of God relate to that ultimate goal of God in this theater? Is the created universe the theater of God? What difference does it make?

IS THE UNIVERSE THE THEATER OF GOD?

I would assume immediately that the answer is yes to the question, *Is the universe the theater of God?* God created the universe as the theater for putting his glory on display. However, it's not that simple. Consider Ephesians 1:4–6. This is the first place I go every time I ask about the ultimate purpose of God in the universe. So here I expect to get help about what the theater of God is.

[God] chose us in him [that is, in Christ] before the foundation of the world, that we should be holy and blameless before him. In love he predestined us for adoption as sons through Jesus Christ, according to the purpose of his will, to the praise of his glorious grace, with which he has blessed us in the Beloved.

THREE REASONS GOD'S THEATER IS BIGGER

Here's the catch. Three times in those verses Paul speaks of the glorious displays of Christ's greatness *before* and *outside* this created universe. So it seems inadequate to say that this created universe is the full extent of the theater of God.

1) Election "before the Foundation of the World"

First, he says in verse 4, "[God] chose us *in him* before the foundation of the world." So our election, before the creation of the world, took place "in Christ." I take that to mean, "in relation to Christ," as well as in Paul's usual sense of union with Christ—not yet existing but known by God in advance. God elects sinners. And they are not contemplated in their election as his apart from their relationship to

---

[6]John Calvin, *Sermons on the Epistle to the Ephesians*, xii.

Christ. Christ is the gracious, undeserved ground of our election before we were created.

So it appears that the theater for displaying the greatness of Christ's role in our salvation includes not just this universe but the eternal scope of God's existence. The theater of God, for the display of the greatness of Christ and his work, is not just the creation of God but the mind of God.

2) Predestination "for Adoption as Sons"

Second, Paul says at the end of verse 4 and into verse 5, "In love he predestined us for adoption as sons *through Jesus Christ*." Predestination happens outside this universe and before it. The predestination of the elect is that they be adopted into the family of God. As Paul said in Romans 8:29, "[We are] predestined to be conformed to the image of his Son, in order that he might be the firstborn among many brothers."

And he makes clear in Ephesians 1:5 that this eternal decision happens "through Jesus Christ." "He predestined us for adoption as sons *through Jesus Christ*." In other words, when God considers making—the very words here are inadequate because there was no "when" before creation—when God decides to make sinners his own children, he only considers it "through Jesus Christ." So already in eternity, the greatness of Christ as mediator is seen.

To be sure, we see it from inside the universe—from inside the created theater of God. But what we are being asked to see is outside of that created theater. The total theater for the greatness of Christ is the eternal intratrinitarian actions of the Godhead.

3) Blessing "in the Beloved"

Third, Paul says in verse 6 that the aim of this election and predestination to adoption is "to the praise of his glorious grace, *with which he has blessed us in the Beloved*." If God's election unto holiness and blamelessness, and his predestination to adoption, lead to the praise of the glory of his grace, it is likely that this grace includes the grace of election and predestination, and not only the grace of atonement through Christ. And this grace, verse 6 says, is "in the Beloved"—that is, in the Son whom the Father loved from all eternity.

So all the grace that was being enacted for us before the theater of the universe was created was enacted "in the Beloved." All God's gracious plans that he conceived for us from eternity were conceived and planned in relation to Christ. And now in the Script for the drama of God's revelation (the Bible), the Author (God) tells us about the glories of the Hero (Christ) as the mediator of grace before the theater was created.

GLORY BEFORE CALVARY—EVEN BEFORE CREATION

Listen to the way Paul confirms this in 2 Timothy 1:9: God "saved us and called us to a holy calling, not because of our works but because of his own purpose and *grace, which he gave us in Christ Jesus before the ages began.*" Grace—undeserved, blood-bought grace—was given to us "before the ages began." And how did he give grace to us before the theater of the universe was created? He gave us grace *in Christ Jesus* before the ages began.

John the apostle adds his confirmation. He pictures this gracious, saving work of God before time and space as the writing of our names in a book. And the name of the book in Revelation 13:8 is "the book of life of the Lamb who was slain." This gives a crimson color to all the glories of Christ before Calvary and even before creation.

THE UNIVERSE IS TOO SMALL AND TOO SHORT

So my conclusion from Ephesians 1:4–6—in answer to the question, *Is the created universe the theater of God?*—is that it is, but the universe is not large enough and long enough to display the fullness of the glories of Christ in the way he works to save sinners and to fill the renewed theater of creation with his glory. The author of the drama of creation and the builder of the theater of the universe must direct our attention back to eternity and outside this universe to find ample scope for the revelation of the glory of the Son.

So when Calvin says in the *Institutes* that "the greater part of mankind . . . walk blindfolded in this glorious theatre,"[7] this is true not only because people don't see the sun and moon and galaxies displaying the glory of God (Ps. 19:1), but even more because they don't look to the wider theater of eternity where God was forever at work electing and predestining and giving grace—all of it in Christ and through Christ and for Christ.

But I have been assuming in what I said, the answers to the questions

---

[7]*Institutes*, 1.5.8

we have not yet answered: What is the ultimate goal of God in the theater of God? How do the historical work and the eternal person of the Son of God relate to the ultimate goal of God in this theater? What difference does it make to us? Let's take those one at a time.

WHAT IS THE ULTIMATE GOAL OF GOD IN THE THEATER OF GOD?

Ephesians 1:4–6 gives the answer.

> [God] chose us in him before the foundation of the world, that we should be holy and blameless before him. In love he predestined us for adoption as sons through Jesus Christ, according to the purpose of his will, *to the praise of the glory of his grace*. [more literal than the ESV's "praise of his glorious grace"]

This is the most ultimate statement of God's purpose in the theater of God—the whole theater both before creation and in creation. The aim of election, the aim of holiness and blamelessness, the aim of predestination and adoption, the aim of bringing all this to pass "through Jesus Christ" is so there would be everlasting, white-hot praise of God's people for "the glory of his grace."

The Glory of His Grace

God has done everything with a view to one great end—namely, that the glory of his grace should be praised by innumerable redeemed human beings. You and everybody you know are commanded to join this ultimate aim of all things in the theater of God (Ps. 96:1–3). You were made to see the glory of God and not feel lukewarm about it (because God spits lukewarmness out of his mouth), but to feel the greatest possible zeal for the glory of God—that is, the beauty of his manifold perfections. And that seeing of God's glory and savoring of God's glory are meant to overflow in expressions of praise for God's glory from your heart and your mind and your voice and your body.

The Glory of Grace Is Ultimate

And, more specifically, Paul says in verse 6, the ultimate glory, the apex of God's glory that you were made to praise, is the glory of his grace. All of his other glories—the glory of his justice and wrath and power and wisdom and truthfulness—serve to make the glory of his grace more plain, more beautiful, and more precious. Here's the way Paul says that in Romans 9:22–23.

> What if God, desiring to show his wrath and to make known his power, has endured with much patience vessels of wrath prepared for destruction, in order to make known the riches of his glory for vessels of mercy, which he has prepared beforehand for glory.

Notice carefully. The revelation of his wrath and his power are penultimate, and the revelation of the riches of his glory for the beneficiaries of mercy is ultimate. In other words, the glory of God's wrath and the glory of God's power ultimately serve in the theater of God to make the glory of his mercy and grace to shine more brightly.

God has done everything—election, predestination, creation, adoption, manifestations of wrath and power and justice and wisdom—all of it to solidify and intensify the praise of his people for the glory of this grace.

And what is that grace whose glory we were created to praise forever with ever-increasing intensity? Or to ask it another way: *What is the love of God?*

What Is the Love of God?

Paul answers later in Ephesians 2:4–7:

> God . . . because of the *great love* with which he loved us, even when we were dead in our trespasses, made us alive together with Christ . . . so that in the coming ages he might *show* the immeasurable riches of his grace in kindness toward us in Christ Jesus.

This word "show" (in "show [Greek *endeixhtai*, from *endeiknumi*] the immeasurable riches of his grace") doesn't merely mean to *treat* with grace and kindness. It means to manifest, display, put forth, demonstrate, prove. The point is that God does all things "for the praise of the glory of [God's] grace" according to Ephesians 1:6, and therefore God is going to spend an eternity of ages *showing* us more and more of the riches of that glory to satisfy our ever-growing capacities to see it and savor it and praise it.

GIVING HIS PEOPLE DELIGHT IN HIMSELF

And Paul calls this "the great love of God." Ephesians 2:4–5 says, "Because of the *great love* with which he loved us" he "made us alive" and opened our eyes and will be showing us more and more of himself forever in the coming ages. So what is *the love of God*? It's *God's commitment to do whatever is necessary to give his people an endless display of himself and endless delight in himself.*

And the person whom we will see and savor and praise forever is a person whose attributes exist in such a way that the apex of his glory is grace.

So, as strange as it sounds, God's grace is what enables us to see his glory and is itself the apex of the glory we see. God has done all things in the theater of God "to the praise of the glory of his grace." And the doing of all things to that end *is* the revelation of grace.

Now we are on the brink of the answer to the next question.

HOW DO THE HISTORICAL WORK AND THE ETERNAL PERSON OF THE SON OF GOD RELATE TO GOD'S ULTIMATE GOAL IN THE THEATER OF GOD?

How do the person and work of Christ relate to God's display of the glory of his grace for the praise of his people? And the answer is: *The historical work of Christ is the action of God's grace, and the eternal person of Christ is the gift of God's grace.* The grace of his work on the cross makes it possible for sinners to enjoy the grace of his person forever.

Jesus is the embodiment of the glory of God's grace, and Jesus is the means of attaining the glory of that grace. God glorifies his grace through the work of Jesus, and Jesus himself is the radiance of that glory (Heb. 1:3). The grace of Christ purchases the ultimately satisfying gift. And the glory of that grace *is* the gift. Jesus is the *way* God gives, as well as *what* God gives. He's the price, and he's the pearl.

Jesus: Both Purchase and Prize

And when you pause to think about it, it must be this way, because for Jesus to be either of these two, he must also be the other. To be either, he must be both. If he is to be the glorious Redeemer who bears our sins and provides our righteousness and purchases our everlasting enjoyment of himself, then he must be the infinitely valuable, all-satisfying revelation of the glory of God. No lesser Redeemer will do.

And turn it around: If he is to be the all-satisfying revelation of the glory of God's grace, then he must be the one who goes to Calvary and performs the greatest work of grace there ever was. So for him to be either the purchase of grace or the prize of grace, he must be both.

The implication of what I am saying is that "the glory of the grace of God" that we are destined to praise forever, according to Ephesians 1:6, is the glory of Christ. That is, the glory of God the Father and the glory of God the Son are one glory. And that glory is the glory of his historical work and the glory of his eternal person.

Confirmation and Illustration

Consider these confirming and illustrating texts:

2 Corinthians 4:4. When God opens our eyes, we see "the light of the gospel of the glory of Christ, who is the image of God." Or as verse 6 says, we have "the light of the knowledge of the glory of God in the face of Jesus Christ." In the gospel, we see the glory of Christ's work, and we inherit the glory of Christ's person. And this glory is the glory of God.

Ephesians 3:21. "To [God] be glory in the church and in Christ Jesus throughout all generations." The glory that we see in God and render to him is "in Christ Jesus."

Philippians 4:19. "My God will supply every need of yours according to his riches in glory in Christ Jesus." The riches of the glory of God are in Christ.

John 12:41. John takes our breath away after quoting Isaiah 6:10 from that famous passage where the prophet says, "Holy, holy, holy . . . the whole earth is full of his glory!" (Isaiah 6:3). He adds, "Isaiah said these things because he saw his [that is, Christ's] glory and spoke of him." How much more plain could John make it that the glory of Yahweh is the glory of Christ?

Which is why James simply calls him "our Lord Jesus Christ, the Lord of glory" (James 2:1), and why Paul calls our blessed hope "the appearing of the glory of our great *God* and Savior Jesus Christ" (Titus 2:13). Jesus is the Lord of glory because he is the "great God and Savior."

So when Ephesians 1:6 says that the entire drama in the entire theater of God has this one great end—"the praise of the glory of the grace of God" through Christ and in the Beloved—he means that the historical *work* of Christ reveals the glory of God's grace as our all-sufficient purchase, and the eternal *person* of Christ reveals the glory of God's grace as our all-satisfying prize. His work is our glorious redemption. His person is our glorious reward.

His role in the theater of God is to display the apex of God's glory in history for our perfect salvation and in eternity for our perfect satisfaction.

Which leaves us with one last question.

WHAT DIFFERENCE DOES IT MAKE FOR US?

We conclude with five practical effects.

1) *Admiration: The Highest of Pleasures*

The highest pleasure of the human being is the pleasure of admiration. Salvation is ultimately the revelation of the glory of Christ in such a way that we can enjoy his greatness and are not destroyed. "Father," Jesus prayed, "I desire that they also, whom you have given me, may be with me where I am, to see my glory that you have given me because you loved me before the foundation of the world" (John 17:24).

To see and savor the glory of Christ—that is, to admire him—is why we were created. Make it your greatest ambition and vocation to see the glory of Christ and say with the apostle Paul, "I count everything as loss because of the surpassing worth of knowing Christ Jesus my Lord" (Phil. 3:8).

2) *New Creation as Nothing Compared to Christ*

When the theater of God is totally renewed and we dwell in the new heavens and new earth, the dazzling creation, ten thousand times more glorious than the sun, will be as nothing compared to Christ himself. Indeed John says, "The city has no need of sun or moon to shine on it, for the glory of God gives it light, and its lamp is the Lamb" (Rev. 21:23). The glory of God through the lamp of the crucified Lamb will be the radiance of the beauty of all things. We will not be pantheists, but we will see Christ in all things, and will see all things by the light of Christ. His beauty will have no competitor.

3) Being Loved by God: Rescued from Self and Enabled to Make Much of Him

Now we understand that to be loved by God is not ultimately to be made much of, but to be rescued from that craving and that bondage, and to be enabled, at great cost, to enjoy making much of God is. As Peter said, "Christ also suffered once for sins, the righteous for the unrighteous, *that he might bring us to God*" (1 Pet. 3:18). This is God's love: God's bringing us to God. Opening our eyes to God. Awakening our affections for God. The apex of God's love is to give us himself for our everlasting enjoyment—and to do it by displaying the glory of Christ as our all-sufficient Rescue and our all-satisfying Reward.

4) Our Glory Reflecting the Glory of Christ

To be sure, we ourselves will be glorified. We will share in his glory. We will shine like the sun in the kingdom of our Father (Matt. 13:43). But when we do, our glory will be the reflected glory of Christ, not our own. "To this he called you," Paul wrote, "through our gospel, so that you may *obtain* the glory of our Lord Jesus Christ" (2 Thess. 2:14).

We *will* be glorious. But the glory will be his. And what will be most glorious about us is that we will be able to see and savor *his* glory with the very passion that the Father himself has for his Son, as Jesus prays in John 17:26, "[May] the love with which you [Father] have loved me . . . be in them, and I in them."

5) Being Changed by Seeing His Glory in the Gospel

When God gives us eyes to see the glory of God in the gospel of Christ, we are gradually changed into the likeness of Christ. "We all, with unveiled face, beholding the glory of the Lord, are being transformed into the same image from one degree of glory to another" (2 Cor. 3:18).

So already now, the age to come—the age of glory—has begun. Redemption is accomplished in Christ. By the Holy Spirit, our eyes are opened to see the light of the gospel of the glory of Christ. And beholding it, we are being changed—a down payment on our final glorification.

And we know that when he comes, our transformation will be complete, and we will be like him, for we will see him as he is (1 John 3:2).

STAND IN AWE OF CHRIST

Therefore, when you get up in the morning and before you go to bed at night, and all day long, with "one foot raised," stand in awe of Christ, the *dénouement* in the theater of God.

APPENDIX ONE
A Note on Calvin & Servetus

Mark R. Talbot

"For many," Bruce Gordon opens his chapter on Calvin and Servetus, "the execution of Michael Servetus in Geneva has defined John Calvin's posthumous reputation. From the sixteenth century to this day detractors have seized this moment as confirmation of his tyrannical, intolerant character."[1]

As I noted near the beginning of my chapter, John Piper asked that my contribution deal with "some of Calvin's own imperfections, notably the Servetus affair," because he wants our treatment of Calvin to be realistic and not a whitewash or cheap hagiography. I have postponed my treatment of this topic until now in part because the more I have read about Calvin's part in Servetus's execution the less attention it seems to merit.

The facts leading up to Servetus's burning at the stake at Champel outside Geneva on October 27, 1553, are these: Michael Servetus, a Spaniard, had been in contact with Calvin for over twenty years. Their theological disagreements began before the publication of Calvin's first theological work, the *Psychopannychia*, since that work "was at least in part," Gordon reports, "directed against views attributed to Servetus and his circle in Paris."[2] In 1531, Servetus published *On the Errors of the Trinity*, which, Roland Bainton observes, "contains both an assault upon the traditional view and a reconstruction of his own position. The former necessitated his withdrawal from Catholic lands; the latter was to make his residence untenable also on Protestant soil."[3] Three years

---

[1]Bruce Gordon, *Calvin* (New Haven: Yale University Press, 2009), 217. Similarly, Selderhuis notes that "Questions as to whether or not Calvin was mentally disturbed, and perhaps even a psychological case, are raised most often in connection with the Servetus affair" (Herman J. Selderhuis, *John Calvin: A Pilgrim's Life* [Downers Grove, IL: InterVarsity, 2009], 203).
[2]Ibid., 217.
[3]Roland H. Bainton, *Hunted Heretic: The Life and Death of Michael Servetus 1511–1553* (Providence, RI: Blackstone Editions, 2005), 13.

later, Calvin took the considerable risk of returning to Paris to meet with Servetus, either—depending on which account we credit—to "gain him for our Savior" or to silence him, but Servetus was a no-show.[4] In 1545, Servetus contacted Calvin again, luring him into correspondence by asking for help in understanding three difficult theological points.[5] Calvin explained them; Servetus disputed Calvin's explanations; Calvin replied again and sent Servetus a copy of his *Institutes* as giving fuller answers. Servetus returned the copy scribbled up with his criticisms, along with part of his yet unfinished *Restoration of Christianity* and some other writings and suggested that he come to Geneva. By this time, Calvin had concluded that Servetus would abandon his heresies only if God changed his heart, and so he warned Servetus not to come.[6] Servetus published his *Restoration* at the beginning of 1553 and sent a copy to Calvin. Its Latin title, *Christianismi Restitutio*, was, Parker writes, "a deliberate hit at [Calvin's] *Institutio*."[7] Calvin found the *Restoration* to be full of errors and "prodigious blasphemies against God"—indeed, "a rhapsody patched up from the impious ravings of all ages."[8] On August 13 of that year, Servetus came to a Sunday service at Calvin's church. When some recognized him, they told Calvin, who took steps to have the civil magistrate arrest him.

By the time Servetus appeared in Geneva, he was already a fugitive from justice, who had been tried and condemned as a heretic to be burned

---

[4]Bainton is my source with the former account when he quotes Calvin's own account of his final interview with Servetus, in ibid., 147; the latter account is Gordon's (*Calvin*, 43), apparently taken from Beza's *Life of Calvin*. Of course, both accounts may reflect part of what was in Calvin's mind when he went to Paris.

[5]Bainton comments that

> Servetus . . . [had] a concern at least for a fellowship of the spirit on earth and wished to gain living converts. Rome would not listen. Basel, Strassburg, and Wittenberg were deaf. But in the meantime a new center of Protestantism had arisen . . . [in] Geneva. . . . Servetus resolved by correspondence to establish that interchange which in the flesh he had missed some years ago in Paris. *Of all the reformers, Calvin appeared to be the one who might be disposed to listen.* (*Hunted Heretic*, 95–96, my emphasis)

[6]Calvin's opinion about Servetus's spiritual state comes out in a letter to John Frellon on 13 February 1546, and Calvin reports his warning to Farel in another letter on the same day. Calvin's words concerning that warning have received a lot of attention, since Calvin said to Farel that "if he comes, I will never let him depart alive, if I have any authority." But Parker observes that those words can be read either "as a threat or as a warning" (T. H. L. Parker, *Portrait of Calvin* [1954; repr. Minneapolis, MN: Desiring God, 2009], 148). If they are a warning, then of course they should not automatically be taken to express a resolution by Calvin to do whatever he could to have Servetus found and killed.

[7]Ibid.

[8]This is in Calvin's letter to the pastors of the church at Frankfurt, dated August 27, 1553. The *Restoration* included a revision of Servetus's earlier work on the Trinity plus several other books that propagated what anyone who is orthodox would take to be egregious errors. In fact, one of the main considerations against Servetus during his trial was, as the ministers of Basel put it, that he "exceeds all the old heretics since he vomits their combined errors from one impudent and blasphemous mouth" (quoted by Bainton, *Hunted Heretic*, 138). For a detailed examination of Servetus's views, see Bainton.

at the stake by the Catholic Inquisition. But in Geneva, the determination of Servetus's fate was entirely in the hands of the civil magistrates.[9] As Gordon notes, "Although Servetus' quarrel was clearly with Calvin, the Frenchman's role in the process was limited."[10] In Servetus's trial before the civil magistrates, Calvin was, as Alister McGrath puts it, a "technical advisor or expert witness, rather than prosecutor."[11] Claude Rigot, the actual prosecutor, was, as Bainton notes, of Geneva's Libertine party—in other words, he was of the party that was made up of "the chief enemies of Calvin"[12]—and, in prosecuting Servetus he "acted in entire independence of Calvin."[13]

What the civil magistrates and Calvin shared was the belief that heresy had to be confronted and punished. Their reasons for holding this belief were probably somewhat different. For Calvin, opposition to heresy was primarily a matter of upholding God's honor: both heresy and blasphemy were affronts to God, and the purpose of confronting and punishing both heretic and blasphemer was "to vindicate the honor of God by silencing those who sully His holy name."[14] On the issue of

---

[9]In setting the context for his examination of Calvin's part in Servetus's trial and execution, Alister McGrath observes, in his *Life of John Calvin*, that

> If there was one area of civic life which the [Geneva] city council was determined to keep totally within its control, it was the administration of justice. The Genevan magistracy had seized the right to administer civil and criminal justice during their revolt against the bishop of Geneva.... In 1527, the right of the bishop to try civil cases was ceded to the city. Over the years which followed, full judicial authority was gradually ceded to Messieurs de Genève: the right to execute criminal sentences was transferred to the syndics, and appeals from within the city to external superior courts were blocked. By 1530, the city had gained total control of the judiciary. *The right to dispense high justice was, in effect, seen as a public demonstration of the city's independence. To allow any foreign power or individual to influence Genevan justice was to erode the city's hard-won sovereignty. There was no way in which Messieurs de Genève were prepared to allow a foreigner [like Calvin] any influence over the central feature of the Genevan civic administration.* (Alister E. McGrath, *A Life of John Calvin* [Oxford: Blackwell, 1990], 114–15, my emphasis)

As Selderhuis notes concerning this same line of civic development, "One might easily draw the conclusion that Calvin was the tyrant of Geneva, but only if one pays no attention to dates. The city, for instance, had already decided to purify itself and adopt imperial law—*including the death-penalty for heretics*—as its norm when Calvin was still many miles away, and in fact still a student" (*John Calvin*, 64, my emphasis).

McGrath's account of "The Servetus Affair" is the best I have encountered, and I urge my readers to acquaint themselves with it.

[10]Gordon, *Calvin*, 219.

[11]McGrath, *Life*, 119.

[12]Bainton, *Hunted Heretic*, 101.

[13]Ibid., 122.

[14]Ibid., 116. These are Bainton's words summarizing Calvin's position. I take the long quotation from Calvin that follows from the next page of Bainton. This is part of Calvin's exposition of Deuteronomy 13. We have access to Calvin's full remarks in his sermons of October 11–21, 1555 in *Sermons on Deuteronomy* (Edinburgh: The Banner of Truth Trust, 1987 [first published in 1583]), 527–52. One of the most important features of these sermons is Calvin's repeated insistence that heresy and blasphemy are worse than crime and thus even more strongly call out for judgment and punishment.

Bainton remarks that "in Calvin's eyes [Servetus] was . . . thrice over a heretic and a blasphemer" because he held heretical views about God, about Christ, and about fallen human nature (117).

whether mercy should be shown to a heretic like Servetus, Calvin thought Christians had no choice, as some of his commentary on Deuteronomy 13 makes clear:

> Those who would spare heretics and blasphemers are themselves blasphemers. Here we follow not the authority of men but we hear God speaking as in no obscure terms He commands His church forever. Not in vain does He extinguish all those affections by which our hearts are softened: the love of parents, brothers, neighbors and friends. He . . . practically denudes men of their nature lest any obstacle impede their holy zeal. Why is such implacable zeal demanded unless that devotion to God's honor should be preferred to all human concerns and as often as His glory is at stake we should expunge from memory our mutual humanity.

For the civil magistrates, the main reason to punish heretics was that their doctrines subverted social order. For instance, Bainton notes that Servetus maintained during his trial that "God would not regard as mortal those sins which are committed before the age of twenty"[15] and that Rigot took this teaching as "a license to the young to commit adultery, theft, and murder with impunity."[16] When Servetus maintained that there had been no criminal prosecution for doctrinal disagreement in the early church and that during Constantine's days heresy deserved no more than banishment, Rigot "replied that Servetus was wrong about the early Church. It was the pagan judges who 'cared for none of these things.' The Christians executed heretics from Constantine to Justinian."[17] Indeed, Servetus's very plea for religious liberty "was interpreted as a political menace, on the ground that it would take the sword of justice from the magistrate."[18]

What the civil and religious authorities probably shared was a belief that tolerating views as aberrant as Servetus's would bring down God's wrath and judgment on those who did so.[19] And what they surely shared

---

[15]Ibid., 128.
[16]Ibid., 129.
[17]Ibid.
[18]Ibid.
[19]See Calvin's *Sermons on Deuteronomy 13*, cited in footnote 14 and this statement in Bainton regarding Rigot's prosecution of Servetus:

> [Rigot's] attempt to connect Servetus with the Jews and the Turks is highly significant in view of the popular belief that tolerance of his views would cause Europe to succumb to the Turks; it was remembered that the regions in which Paul of Samosata and Arius had once assailed the Trinity [in ways very similar to Servetus's arguments] were now in the hands of the infidel (Ibid., 129–30).

was a belief that not to execute Servetus, if he did not repent and retract his views, would make the Protestant territories seem dangerously soft both religiously and politically. This was the common sentiment of all of the Swiss cities when the civil magistrates of Geneva polled them on how they should treat Servetus. For instance, Zurich responded that Geneva "should work against him with great faith and diligence especially as our churches have an ill repute abroad as heretics and patrons of heretics. God's holy providence has now indeed provided this occasion whereby you may at once purge yourselves and us from this fearful suspicion of evil."[20]

A careful consideration of Calvin's part in Servetus's arrest, trial, and execution makes it clear, then, that Servetus's fate is not "confirmation of [Calvin's] tyrannical, intolerant character." Gordon, whom we have already seen to be more than willing to highlight Calvin's faults, stresses that while Calvin took heresy to be a capital offense, he wanted "Servetus to recant, not die."[21] And, indeed, when the sentence was passed that Servetus would be burned at the stake, Calvin tried to get the mode of execution changed to either beheading by sword or hanging because either would be less painful and thus more humane.

Servetus's fate, then, should not be attributed to an imperfection unique to Calvin. In measure we may chastise Calvin along with his century with the advantage of our five hundred-year hindsight, but insofar as we recoil against what happened to Servetus, we must recoil against what was primarily an imperfection of Calvin's century. As McGrath summarizes it:

> Sadly, every major Christian body which traces its history back to the six-teenth century has blood liberally scattered over its credentials. Roman Catholic, Lutheran, Reformed and Anglican: all have condemned and executed their Servetuses. . . . It is fair to suggest that it is improper to single out Calvin as if he were somehow the initiator of this vicious trend, or a particularly vigorous and detestable supporter of the practice, where the majority of his enlightened contemporaries wished it to be abolished. The case of Etienne Le Court, who was publicly degraded, strangled and burned by the Inquisition at Rouen on 11 December 1533, for suggesting that, among other things, 'women will preach the gospel,' would seem considerably more disturbing.

---

[20]Ibid., 138.
[21]Gordon, *Calvin*, 223.

"Perhaps historians," McGrath concludes, "like everyone else, have their axes to grind."[22] To target Calvin the way that he has been targeted for his part in the Servetus affair should, McGrath observes, raise "difficult questions concerning the precommitments of his critics." For "Servetus was the *only* individual put to death for his religious opinions in Geneva during Calvin's lifetime, at a time when executions of this nature were a commonplace elsewhere."[23] In other words, Servetus's execution in Geneva is less attributable to Calvin as a particularly bad actor than to Europe's sixteenth-century culture as a temporal manifestation of our world's broken stage.

Calvin had many faults, but to deny that his part in the Servetus affair is to be taken as a particularly egregious example of some of them is not to involve ourselves in a whitewash or some sort of cheap hagiography. Pastor Piper is, indeed, right that this is an issue that I, with my topic, needed to address, even if ultimately it is one that we can lay to rest.

---

[22]McGrath, *Life*, 120.
[23]Ibid., 116.

APPENDIX TWO

The Life & Ministry of
John Calvin—A Brief Biography

David Mathis

Over five hundred years ago now, on July 10, 1509, he was born Jean Cauvin in Noyon, France—about seventy miles north of Paris. His father was Gerard, son of a barrelmaker and boatman. Gerard was a lawyer, and it was his law practice that brought him into the everyday sphere of the church.

The young Jean benefitted immensely through his father's ecclesiastical connections. He was able to be educated privately with the children of the wealthy Montmor family and eventually garnered church support for his further studies.

Gérard originally planned a career for his son in the church. But when things later soured with the dioceses, he would redirect his son toward law.

When Martin Luther nailed his Ninety-five Theses to the church door in Wittenberg on October 31, 1517, and unknowingly launched the Reformation in earnest, the young Calvin was a mere eight years old. He likely heard very little, if anything, about the rebellious German monk until Jean left for university in Paris at age fourteen. There he would hear more.

OFF TO PARIS (1523–1532)
It was 1523, when Calvin arrived at university. Providentially, he didn't need to leave home alone but went with two of the Montmor sons.

In Paris, Calvin learned Latin from the respected Mathurin Cordier, who decades later would teach at the academy Calvin would found in Geneva. Under Cordier's instruction, the young Calvin became aware of

John Wycliffe, Jan Hus, Martin Luther, and the ongoing Reformation. At Paris he earned both a BA and MA.

Meanwhile back in Noyon, his father Gérard's relationship with the dioceses was strained to the breaking point. Stiff-armed by the church, Gérard, who had originally encouraged his son toward a career in the ministry, now prodded his son away from theological studies toward law.

In 1528, at his father's request, Calvin left his theological studies in Paris to pursue law at Orléans. He was there almost a year, then left for Bourges for three more years of study in law. In Bourges, Calvin was surrounded by the best of humanism, but church historian Justo Gonzalez writes, "At the very time when he was profoundly imbued in the spirit of humanism, Calvin felt no admiration for the vacuous elegance that characterized some of the most famous humanists."[1]

Calvin's growing disillusionment with humanism brought him to the brink of his conversion. Church historians argue about when he may have experienced the new birth—a debate we don't need to enter here. Suffice it to say Calvin seems to have been converted sometime between 1528 and 1532.

In 1531, his father Gérard died, and Calvin found himself free from his father's request that he study law. Calvin was twenty-two years old, and his desires were changing. So he returned to Paris to study theology. But soon he would be on the run.

DE CLEMENTIA, CONVERSION, AND COP (1532–1535)

It was 1532, at age twenty-three, when Calvin published his first book, a commentary on Seneca's *De Clementia*. He hoped it would make for a celebrated inauguration to the guild, but it didn't sell as he dreamed.

In 1533, now some sixteen years after Luther posted his Ninety-five Theses (and inadvertently launched the Reformation), Calvin was in Paris, certainly now converted and a Protestant. His friend Nicolas Cop delivered a catalytic All Saints' Day convocation address at the University of Paris. He heralded Christ as the sole mediator, not Mary or any "saint." The address, supposedly written by Calvin in part, meant Calvin and Cop had to flee town for their livelihood.

---

[1]Justo L. Gonzalez, *The Story of Christianity* (Peabody, MA: Prince Press), 2:62.

Still in exile from Paris in January 1535, Calvin went to Basel where he would write and publish his first edition of his *Institutes of the Christian Religion.*

INSTITUTES (1535–1536)

Calvin wrote as a fugitive. Exiled from France, he eventually settled in Basel where he found enough space and leisure to put together the first edition of his *Institutes of the Christian Religion.*

The first edition debuted in March 1536 and was a relatively short book—nothing close to the one thousand-plus pages of the final edition. The first edition was designed to be small enough to fit into a minister's coat pocket so it could be carried and referenced at any time in any place.

He would later write, "All I had in mind was to hand on some elementary teaching by which anyone who had been touched by an interest in religion might be formed to true godliness. I labored at the task especially for our own Frenchmen, for I saw that many were hungering and thirsting after Christ and yet that only a very few had any real knowledge of him." Amazing that this elementary teaching would grow into one of the most important books in the history of the church.

Three years later in 1539, with Calvin now in Strasbourg (having been exiled from Geneva), he saw fit to make updates and produce the second edition of his *Institutes.*

The first two editions appeared in Latin. But in 1541 Calvin himself undertook to translate the second-edition Latin into his native French. From here, his translating a new Latin edition into French became a practice he would attend to for each following publication of the *Institutes* until his death.

The third edition came in 1543, then a fourth edition seven years later in 1550.

Finally, during the winter of 1558, Calvin's health was rapidly deteriorating, and he thought himself at death's doorstep. (He would actually recover and live until 1564.) So once again he undertook the significant task of revising his *Institutes.* Anticipating this would be his last edition (which it proved to be), he poured all he had into making it final and definitive. His French translation came out in 1660, and Calvin's *Institutes* was complete.

A NIGHT'S STAY IN GENEVA (1536–1538)

William Farel was the fiery redhead who cursed Calvin's ivory-tower life in Strasbourg and twisted his arm to stay in Geneva. Here's the story.

Having published his *Institutes*, which were immediately successful, Calvin left Basel, still a fugitive from France, in the summer of 1536 to make for Strasbourg where he could pursue a life of study and writing while tucked away under the pastoral care of famed reformer Martin Bucer. (Bucer had come to the Reformed faith after seeing Martin Luther defend his emerging Protestant doctrine at the Heidelberg Disputation in 1518.)

However, Calvin and his traveling companions (which included his brother Antoine) discovered that the direct way between Basel and Strasbourg was blocked by the troops of Charles V as he was fighting the latest installment of the Hapsburg-Valois war with France's Francis I. So Calvin and company had to pursue the indirect route, which meant stopping for a night—just a single night—in Geneva.

That evening word got to William Farel that the author of the *Institutes* was staying in town. Farel was the first reformer of Geneva. He was the pioneer who fought to have the city become officially Protestant in May 1536. But now a year in, he needed help. And Calvin's gift mix seemed to complement his perfectly.

He descended upon Calvin and pled that he stay in Geneva and partner with him in bringing the Reformation there into fullness. Calvin resisted. He saw himself more as an academic than a pastor. He longed to hide away in Strasbourg and write books that would help the Reformation across Europe.

When he saw he was making no headway with Calvin, Farel pronounced a curse, damning Calvin's quiet studies in Strasbourg when the need was so acute in Geneva. Amazingly, Calvin conceded. Whether it was fear of God or the effect of Farel's display of earnestness, we don't know for sure. Maybe both.

So Calvin remained in Geneva, and by January 1537 he and Farel were fully engaged in their attempt to complete the Reformation in Geneva. But by Easter of the following year, they hit a major snag. The Reformers were expelled from Geneva.

THE GOLDEN YEARS (1538-1541)

Calvin spent the happiest years of his life outside Geneva. It started in April 1538 when Calvin and fellow reformer William Farel were expelled.

Their eager reforms were moving more quickly than the city council was ready for. Tensions escalated. Calvin in his youth and Farel in his zeal wouldn't back down, and the council eventually expelled them. It wasn't Calvin's first or last mistake in ministry, but it likely served more than most in breaking the idealistic theologian into a more realistic pastor.

Calvin first went to Basel and then settled in Strasbourg where Bucer was pastoring. After much entreating—and threatening that Calvin's reluctance was like Jonah's!—Bucer prevailed upon him to pastor the "small" French congregation of about five hundred.

While in Strasbourg in 1539, Calvin wrote his memorable response to Cardinal Sadoleto on Geneva's behalf. Seeing that Geneva had expelled its Reformers, Sadoleto wrote to the city in an effort to win her back to the Catholic Church. With Calvin gone, Geneva had no one with enough theological apparatus to adequately answer the Cardinal. So they turned to their exiled Reformer. The relationship was on the mend.

In August 1540, Calvin married Idelette de Bure, widow of an Anabaptist who had been converted to the Reformed faith under Calvin's ministry. Idelette brought to the marriage two children—Jacques and Judith. Calvin and Idelette would be married eight and a half years before her untimely death.

On September 13, 1541, Calvin's "golden years" came to an end. Geneva asked him to return. He was not eager, to say the least, but he felt constrained that it was God's will that he do so. When Calvin returned to the pulpit, he resumed his exposition of the Psalms, picking up at the very place he had been preaching before the exile.

RETURN TO GENEVA (1541-1553)

Now Calvin was back and would settle in for life, in the Geneva for which he would be famous.

Severe trials would come the following year in the form of sickness and death. The plague that had come through Strasbourg now swept through Geneva. Calvin refused to abandon his flock and seek safety outside town, risking his life to remain and comfort his ailing parishioners.

Then in the summer of 1542, Calvin's only child was born and died only two weeks later. It was a great blow. He wrote to his close friend Viret, "The Lord has certainly inflicted a severe and bitter wound in the death of our baby son. But He is Himself a Father and knows best what is good for His children."

Calvin's wife would have no more children and would remain sickly until her death in the spring of 1549. Upon her death, Calvin again wrote to Viret:

> You know well how tender, or rather soft, my mind is. Had not a powerful self-control been given to me, I could not have borne up so long. And truly, mine is no common source of grief. I have been bereaved of the best companion of my life, of one who, had it been so ordained, would have willingly shared not only my poverty but even my death.
>
> During her life she was the faithful helper of my ministry. From her I never experienced the slightest hindrance. She was never troublesome to me throughout the whole course of her illness, but was more anxious about her children than about herself.
>
> As I feared these private worries might upset her to no purpose, I took occasion three days before she died, to mention that I would not fail in discharging my duty towards her children.[2]

Other troubles would come from extended family. In 1548, the wife of his brother Antoine was imprisoned on suspected adultery and soon released. Nine years later she would be convicted of adultery with Calvin's manservant. The Calvin home was no stranger to scandal.

Yet the year 1549 brought not only the darkness of Idelette's death, but an ecclesiastical bright spot. Calvin and Heinrich Bullinger (Zwingli's successor) drew up the Consensus of Zurich, which united the Swiss Reformed churches, bringing together two of the strongest early streams of Reformed theology and laying the foundation for what we still call the *Reformed* church today.

THE FATEFUL YEARS (1553–1554)

T. H. L. Parker calls 1553–1554 Calvin's "fateful years." According to Parker, this was when "two large storms blew from different quarters and raged simultaneously."[3] One was Calvin's battle with the libertines; the other was the infamous Servetus affair.

---

[2]T. H. L. Parker, *Portrait of Calvin* (1954; repr., Minneapolis, MN: Desiring God, 2009), 80.
[3]Ibid.

The Genevan air was charged in the fall of 1553. It was September 3 when the confrontation with the libertines reached its climax, and it was October 26–27 when Michael Servetus was condemned and burned at the stake.

First, the libertines. A pack of unregenerate Genevans—also members of the church in Calvin's magisterial (and non-credobaptist) context—stirred up the trouble. Despite their love of license and open embrace of immorality, they desired good standing in the church and to eat from the Lord's Table.

Calvin, on the other hand, called for discipline and was emphatic that they could not share in Communion without repentance from their sinful patterns. However, the city council sided with the libertines and ordered the church to serve them the Supper. But Calvin wouldn't budge.

The showdown came on September 3—Calvin and the church versus the libertines and the city. The lead libertine was supposed to be in attendance. Calvin fenced the Table and held his ground. Stories vary as to precisely when and how he uttered the memorable line, "These hands you may crush, these arms you may lop off, my life you may take, my blood is yours, you may shed it; but you shall never force me to give holy things to the profaned, and dishonor the table of my God."[4]

Theodore Beza, Calvin's successor in Geneva and first biographer, notes, "After this the sacred ordinance was celebrated with a profound silence, and under solemn awe in all present, as if the Deity Himself had been visible among them."[5]

It turns out the libertines weren't in attendance. Direct confrontation was avoided, and Calvin proved the victor. The libertine head was severed, but the body would continue to convulse—and would be given strength by the Servetus affair to follow.

Michael Servetus was a Spaniard. Quite the Renaissance man, he was a medical doctor, lawyer, and theologian—though he was least gifted theologically. Thus the trouble. About Servetus, Parker comments, "He should have been born three hundred years later. He would have been happy and quite safe in the free-thinking circles of England in the middle of the nineteenth century."[6]

---

[4] Henry F. Henderson, *Calvin in His Letters* (London: J.M. Dent, 1989), 78–79.
[5] Ibid.
[6] Parker, *Portrait*, 105.

The problem was that his doctrine of the Trinity (or lack thereof) was heretical, and he was influential. He had written to Calvin as early as 1545 because of Calvin's international reputation as a theologian, presumably seeking help. Calvin corresponded with Servetus and even risked his life to meet with him in Paris, but Servetus skipped out on the appointment.

By 1553, Servetus was in prison in Spain, awaiting his execution by the Catholics for his denial of the Trinity, when he escaped and eventually appeared in Geneva. When he was recognized, the city arrested him and tried him for heresy.

Servetus was condemned on October 26, 1553, and was burned at the stake the following day. The details are sketchy, but some historians recount that Calvin took great pity on Servetus, visited him in prison, and pled with him to renege on his beliefs and embrace the triune God. Calvin also seems to have asked for a lighter penalty for him in some form—whether it was no death penalty or to grant mercy by strangling him before the burning is not fully clear. It was likely the latter.

Calvin's opponents in Geneva, the libertines chief among them, played up the Servetus affair against him, and it remains the major blight on his character today. And to an extent for good reason. Yes, his role and the depths of depravity he manifested in the affair have likely been exaggerated by his detractors, but we Calvin admirers should be honest enough to say that he messed up. (After all, shouldn't we of all people believe in depravity?)

In going along with the ecclesiastical and judicial procedures and the seeming inevitability of Servetus's fate, Calvin didn't attempt to stop the state from wielding its sword for the church in the convoluted relationship between the two. He sinned—as have all our heroes, but One.

Calvin failed us—and not just in the Servetus affair. So like Luther and Edwards and Spurgeon, his virtue lies in pointing us beyond himself to the One who never failed and took our failures on himself.

No matter his level and depth of involvement, Calvin would no doubt be eager for our Servetus story to end here: Calvin, too, was a great sinner in a need of a great Savior.

AN UNMARKED GRAVE (1554–1564)

Calvin fell deathly ill in the winter of 1558 at age forty-nine. He thought himself at death's doorstep and so turned his few remaining energies to his final revision of his *Institutes*. Until this time, he hadn't been fully pleased with the shape and content of his often-revised magnum opus. Wanting to leave the church with a definitive edition, he worked feverishly, despite the fever, to finish.

His health returned in the spring of 1559, and he soon returned to the pulpit. It was at this time that Denis Raguenier began taking extended shorthand notes on Calvin's sermons, since he didn't prepare manuscripts but preached extemporaneously. The sermon manuscripts of Calvin we have today are largely owing to Raguenier's unflagging and far-sighted labors.

Also in 1559, Calvin and sidekick Theodore Beza founded the Academy of Geneva. Beza would serve as its day-in, day-out head, and the Academy would become famous across Europe and produce lasting effects long after Calvin's death.

In his final five years, he translated the final edition of the *Institutes* into French, wrote a large commentary on the Pentateuch, and preached and lectured almost tirelessly. Almost. At barely fifty years old he was battling increasing illness and frailty, but his labors continued unceasing. There were seasons of sickness followed by renewed strength.

The great Reformer began slowing for the final time in February 1564. Soon it was too draining to preach and lecture. He spent his final months bedridden and died May 27, 1564, just weeks shy of his fifty-fifth birthday.

Calvin could tell in his lifetime that he'd likely be remembered long after his death. So he took pains to fade as namelessly from this world as he could. He requested burial in an unmarked grave hoping to prevent pilgrims from coming to see his resting place and engaging in the kind of idolatry he'd spent his lifetime standing against.

In death he completed his life's labors, not seeking to make much of Calvin, but striving with all his might to point beyond himself to the One who saved him and was his greatest joy—the only One most worthy of being made much of.

ACKNOWLEDGMENTS

Tremendous thanks to eagle-eyes Ted Griffin and Mike Hurley. Now retired, Ted is still contracting with Crossway. For years he has brought his astounding skills to the Piper editorial process. As hard as we try to send Ted a flawless manuscript, he still finds dozens of typos and stylistic infidelities that lesser men have overlooked. And Mike, super-volunteer with Desiring God, is ever ready to lend his care to staring down another manuscript.

Sincere thanks to Carol Steinbach and her team of indexers from Desiring God. Carol has been indexing books about as long as John has been writing them. It's Carol and her aides who make these books searchable by Scripture and person.

Additional thanks to Scott Anderson, who once again oversaw the Desiring God National Conference where these chapters were originally presented. We know of no emcee like Scott. What a gift to us and to thousands of conference-goers.

Heartfelt thanks to the leadership at Crossway—particularly Lane Dennis, Allan Fisher, and Justin Taylor—who agreed to publish this book and who share our vision for gospel-soaked materials that build up the body of Christ. Season after season, no one puts together the outstanding catalog that Crossway does. God has been kind to this company. May he continue to pour out his grace on, and through, Crossway.

Massive thanks to Noël Piper and Megan Mathis. Without their care, support, love, and strength—and long-suffering with our travel—there would be no Desiring God and no *With Calvin in the Theater of God*.

Ultimate thanks go to Jesus, who "loved us and gave himself up for us" (Eph. 5:2). It will be "far better" to soon be in his immediate presence (Phil. 1:23). Nothing compares to "the surpassing worth of knowing Christ Jesus my Lord" (Phil. 3:8). He is the most important J. C. The namesake of this book quickly fades in the light of Jesus' glory and grace.

David Mathis
Twin Cities, Minnesota
Cinco de Mayo, 2010

SUBJECT INDEX

PERSON INDEX

SCRIPTURE INDEX

desiringGod

If you would like to further explore the vision of God and life presented in this book, we at Desiring God would love to serve you. We have hundreds of resources to help you grow in your passion for Jesus Christ and help you spread that passion to others. At our website, desiringGod.org, you'll find almost everything John Piper has written and preached, including more than thirty books. We've made over twenty-five years of his sermons available free online for you to read, listen to, download, and in some cases watch.

In addition, you can access hundreds of articles, find out where John Piper is speaking, learn about our conferences, discover our God-centered children's curricula, and browse our online store. John Piper receives no royalties from the books he writes and no compensation from Desiring God. The funds are all reinvested into our gospel-spreading efforts. Desiring God also has a whatever-you-can-afford policy, designed for individuals with limited discretionary funds. If you'd like more information about this policy, please contact us at the address or phone number below. We exist to help you treasure Jesus Christ and his gospel above all things because he is most glorified in you when you are most satisfied in him. Let us know how we can serve you!

Desiring God
Post Office Box 2901 Minneapolis, Minnesota 55402
888.346.4700 mail@desiringGod.org